HENRY VII

by Charles Williams

the apocryphile press
BERKELEY, CA
www.apocryphile.org

apocryphile press
BERKELEY, CA

Apocryphile Press
1700 Shattuck Ave #81
Berkeley, CA 94709
www.apocryphile.org

First published by Arthur Baker, Ltd. in 1937.
First Apocryphile edition, 2007.

For sale in the USA only. Sales prohibited in the UK.
Printed in the United States of America.

ISBN 1-933993-04-9

PREFACE

ANYONE who has had to read in the history of the Tudor Age finds his attention turned, sooner or later, to the person of King Henry VII. So much began with him—much that lasted, and much that did not last. But who was he that began it all? There are studies: Miss Temperley's learned and lucid account of the reign, Dr. Busch's even more learned and a little less lucid. Of shorter articles the most illuminating are those by Dr. Conyers Read and Dr. C. H. Williams. Even so, the reader is left a little defeated.

To have some notion of Elizabeth, Mary, and Henry VIII, and none of their father and grandfather, is merely tiresome. This book is a personal effort to avoid that tiresomeness. The mere difficulty of discovering Henry as a person makes him attractive, and the unspecialized reader may find matter of interest—such as the translation of Prince Henry's protest against his marriage with Katherine of Aragon—and a more artistic interest in the picture of a King, who, having built a great edifice of monarchy, and peering about it with a candle to provide against cracks, set light to a train of powder that shattered it.

Francis Bacon—and wherever Francis Bacon went future travellers have to learn from him—said of Henry VII that his nature and his fortune so ran together that no man could distinguish between them. The full distinction (which is what all biography tries to effect) may perhaps never be drawn. This is at least a conjecture.

If I say that the responsibility for the book is partly Mr. Arthur Barker's, it is only to make an opportunity of offering a gratitude for a continued kindness and goodwill not only in relation to King Henry VII but in many incidents of the last few years.

CONTENTS

		PAGE
PREFACE		v

CHAPTER
I. "That most Innocent Ympe".		1
II. "Change of Worlds hath caused Change of Mind".		32
III. The King and the Kings		58
IV. The Multiplication of the King		88
V. "He of York"		103
VI. The Marriages		139
VII. The King in His State		166
VIII. The Hunting of Suffolk		185
IX. The Nature of the King		210
X. The Conclusion		259
Biographical Note		266
Index.		267

CHAPTER I

"That most Innocent Ympe"

He began by being, on both sides, almost a bastard. His mother's grandfather had been John of Gaunt; his father's mother had been Katherine of Valois, widow of Henry V. John of Gaunt's legitimatized granddaughter Margaret Beaufort had married Katherine's legitimatized son Edmund Tudor. Henry was their only child.

The marriage in after years was said by St. John Fisher, on the authority of Margaret herself, to have been directed by supernatural power. She had been, a little before her ninth birthday, offered a choice between two bridegrooms, one of whom was Edmund. She had been in some doubt and had taken her difficulty to a friend, a pious old lady, who had told her how St. Nicholas was "the helper of all true maidens," and had advised her to invoke his aid. At about four in the morning of the day when she was to decide, the saint, in episcopal vestments, had appeared to her, and told her to take Edmund for her husband. She obeyed; she "inclined her mind" to Edmund, and so (said Fisher) became the ancestress of kings. This had seemed unlikely at the time, for the legal instrument that had corrected the birth of his mother's house, called Beaufort, and put them within the law, had particularly separated them from the Throne. An act of Richard II and again of Henry IV had declared the Beauforts capable of everything except the royal dignity. Nor on the other side could the relationship carry any claim. Katherine of Valois had married—if she had married— an unknown man, a Welshman, a hanger-on of the Court, Owen Tudor. It had been something of a scandal. Certainly the Tudor professed a descent that made Valois and Plantagenet seem upstarts; he said he sprang from the original kings of Britain, Cadwallader and the rest. Edmund, the son of Owen and Katherine, abandoned the arms of that pre-historic house in favour of a more modern shield, quartering the arms of England and France. It was at once a less modest and a more modest display. He had been brought up with his half-brother, the son of Henry V, who had already become Henry VI, and he enjoyed that King's favour, so long as the King had favours to grant. Edmund died, still young, in 1456.

The wars of the Roses were then a threat to the land. In the preceding year the first skirmish had taken place at St. Albans, and the King had fallen into the hands of the Duke of York, but serious fighting did not begin till 1459, and not

"THAT MOST INNOCENT YMPE" 3

until 1460 did the Duke make his own public claim to the Throne. At St. Albans the Earl of Somerset, also a Beaufort and their chief, had been killed. There had been whispers that Henry VI had intended to make Somerset heir-presumptive, in spite of the legal disability. The suggestion was unpopular, doubly so because Somerset was regarded as responsible for the loss of English territory in France, but also unpopular in itself. The whole idea did no good to the Beauforts or indeed to the Crown.

Margaret Beaufort, who was then not quite fourteen, had taken or been taken to refuge with her husband's relations in Wales. His brother, Jasper Tudor, who had fought at St. Albans, was Earl of Pembroke, and lord of Pembroke Castle. There, towards the end of January 1456–7, her child was born—probably on 28th January, and there for some years he remained, slowly discovering who he was, and how for all the panoply of three royalties—Welsh, English, and French—that danced about him, he was, when it came to the point, no one very particular. His mother, before he was four and she eighteen, had left him to Jasper in Pembroke, and had married again; her new husband was the Lord Stafford, a son of the Duke of Buckingham. It left him by himself then, but it was to be of use later.

The child's legal misfortunes were not ended with his birth. The Roses pranced bloodily over the land, and were marked more and more by actions of personal hate. "The war," in Mr. Belloc's phrase, "was becoming a violent vendetta of reciprocal murder." The Duke of York and his young son were shamefully killed in 1460. In 1461 Henry's grandfather, Owen, who was still alive, and his uncle Jasper of Pembroke, led a force westward in support of the Queen, Margaret of Anjou. They marched to Mortimer's Cross, where on 2nd February they met a much more brilliant captain, Edward Plantagenet, now Duke of York, by succession to his murdered father, and they were utterly defeated. Owen Tudor was taken prisoner and promptly executed; his head, adorned with candles, was set up at Hereford. Jasper escaped from the battle and fled to Scotland. Edward Plantagenet proclaimed himself King, and was crowned at Westminster. Henry VI was captured and confined in the Tower. Edward proceeded to attaint his chief enemies; among them Jasper Tudor in exile, and the small Henry Tudor in Pembroke. His inherited title of Richmond was formally bestowed on Edward IV's brother, George, Duke of Clarence. Nevertheless, for some time the child remained in Lancastrian hands. The castle of Pembroke held out, and before it fell Henry had been transferred to Harlech. Harlech, the last stronghold of Lancaster, was taken at last by Lord Herbert on King Edward's

"THAT MOST INNOCENT YMPE" 5

behalf in 1466, and the boy with it. Herbert became the Yorkist Earl of Pembroke in place of the attainted Jasper, and was given the wardship of the captive and attainted Henry.

At the age of nine, therefore, the boy could have no concern with the Crown; he was a minor, of one of the attainted houses of English nobility, and hereditarily debarred at that from all legal pretence to majesty. What he could hardly have known was the extent to which the prestige of the Crown was beginning to be shaken. The accession of Edward IV might have improved matters, for Edward, if he had any claim at all, had a stronger claim than had his prisoner Henry VI. But alternations of occupancy were bound to shake stable allegiance, and in 1467 another reversal of fortune drove out Edward and brought back Henry VI. The new Earl of Pembroke had been thinking of marrying his ward to his own daughter, but before anything had been done about it the Lancastrians rose, and at Banbury, defeated, captured, and executed him. Jasper Tudor, who had been moving about between Scotland and France, recovered possession of his nephew, and brought him up to London.

In London Henry was presented to the saintly and unfortunate King, whose fate was, as it were, a sacrifice for the rebellion of his grandfather Henry IV against Richard II. It was afterwards said that the King, contemplating the high carriage of the son of his half-brother, was moved to prophecy : " This truly, this is he unto whom both we and our adversaries must yield and give over the dominion." A hundred years later, writing under the established sovereignty of that boy's granddaughter Elizabeth, Shakespeare, practising his own young technique, turned the doubtful story to verse.

> KING HENRY. My Lord of Somerset, what youth is that
> Of whom you seem to have so tender care?
> SOMERSET. My liege, it is young Henry, Earl of Richmond.
> KING HENRY. Come hither, England's hope : If secret powers
> Suggest but truth to my divining thoughts,
> This pretty lad will prove our country's bliss.
> His looks are full of peaceful Majesty,
> His head by nature fram'd to wear a crown,
> His hand to wield a sceptre, and himself
> Likely in time to bless a regal throne.
> Make much of him, my lords ; for this is he
> Must help you more than you are hurt by me.

At least, Henry's attainder was reversed, with those of all other Lancastrians ; he was again Earl of Richmond. It was 1470, and he was thirteen, a person of standing, old enough to take part in affairs, old enough to be decided. His health, during that disturbed boyhood, had not been good ; on the other hand, it was asserted that his tutors had been astonished at his quickness. If it were true, it was because he had had, so far, no need to disguise his quickness; he could let himself be known to be swiftly apprehensive. But, like Elizabeth after him at something the same age, the chief thing he had to apprehend, now and for long, was his own safety. All else depended on that.

The year which followed that momentary sun of the Red Rose's winter saw the White Rose snowing down again, and the young Earl fleeing from the storm. It was the year of the return of Edward IV, of Warwick's defeat at Barnet and Queen Margaret's at Tewkesbury, of the fourteen-year triumph of York. The organized forces of Lancaster were completely overthrown; the Prince of Wales was stabbed after the battle of Tewkesbury; King Henry was murdered on the night of Edward's return to London. Jasper Tudor, after the presentation in London, had gone back to Wales. There, as soon as he heard of the queen's landing, he had raised forces to join her. He had set out with them on his way to Tewkesbury, and had passed Chepstow, when he heard of the grand defeat. He retired on Chepstow, then again back to Pembroke. There King Edward's Welsh allies besieged him under a leader called Morgan Thomas. But in a few days Morgan's brother David came down against him with another force to support Jasper—it is an epigram of those wars—and raised the siege. Jasper could not see anywhere a point of stability for himself or his friends. His sister-in-law, Henry's mother Margaret, sent to him urging him to save her son; delay and capture were growing more dangerous to life with each successive change in the holder of the Crown. A child of four might have escaped what now a boy—a young man —of fourteen might not; the Prince of Wales had been only seventeen when he was stabbed. Jasper consented; he and his nephew fled to Tenby, and then oversea.

Henry had thus escaped the Restoration, but he was an exile. But also, whether or not he or any realized it during that short voyage, he was becoming by now *the* exile. Illegitimate as regards the Crown, attainted as regards his earldom, fugitive as regards his person, it was yet true that he was by now the only likely head of the Lancastrian party. He was the nearest thing to royalty that, if it survived, it possessed. Whether it would survive was another question, but Henry's own survival was its best chance. It is impossible that he should not have seen it. He was a hope. But he showed no immediate eagerness to be regarded as a hope; he was more concerned with his simple survival, and the more he became a hope the less likely was he to be a survival.

Refugees of royalty were common in Europe. It was generally a little difficult to say accurately at any moment what the exact standing of any of them was. Between two mornings a guest of such a kind might become a hostage or even a prisoner; he might, on the other hand, be proposed as a claimant and supported as a Pretender. Henry's ship drew in to Brittany; he was brought to the Duke. He became immediately a piece on the board of a different game. He might be the rising head of the Lancastrians, but that Red castle was now to be pushed about in the moves of a conflict with which in Pembroke they had been little concerned. It was a conflict of more importance to the future history of Europe than the English wars; it was to decide to what extent France should be a nation. The future of France has been ever since what that decision made it.

The Government of France was concerned in a task similar to that of the Government of Spain, and to what was presently to be the task of the Government of England. It was recovering and consolidating territory; it was abolishing feudal lordships of independent power and uncertain loyalty; it was discovering and stabilizing its strength; it was recreating its King. Over the Pyrenees the joined powers of Ferdinand of Aragon and Isabella of Castile were attempting the same thing against the Moorish settlements as well as the Spanish divisions. But in France there were no Moors; there were only duchies and counties, which by one method or another were falling more and more into the power of the French King. The northern parts had been recovered by war in the time of Henry VI, after the great initiative of St. Joan of Arc. Anjou, Maine, Provence, and Burgundy were, or were in process of being, obtained by one device or another. There remained only the Duchy of Brittany and the English city of Calais.

The immediate pressure of the French Government was now maintained against Brittany. Against that pressure the Duke of Brittany had two chief weapons—his soldiers and his two daughters, whose marriages to suitable husbands might procure him more soldiers. The arrival of Henry provided him with the hope of another weapon, or of the means at least to procure other weapons. Henry found himself hospitably received, but it became clear to him, as to all such refugees, that he could not tell from day to day what was the exact nature of the smiles on the faces of his hosts, or how much of promise mingled with how much of pretence. It was a lesson he did not forget when, in later years, he himself was threatened, or in a narrowing mind believed himself to be threatened, by claimants from foreign shelters.

The King of England, the now firmly established Edward Plantagenet, opened correspondence with the Duke of Brittany. He was at that time in alliance with the other great Duchy of Burgundy and in hostility to France under Louis XI. Louis bought him off, but he was still desirous, if possible, to recover the person of Henry, so-called Earl of Richmond. He was aware that Henry "was the only person to disturb all his felicity," though Henry's chances of doing so were small and Henry's claims to do so were smaller. Allegiance in these last months of revolt and re-revolt, of rebellions and treacheries and murders, had come to mean almost nothing. Edward maintained a pressure on the Duke to surrender his guest. The Duke had not so great an objection to surrendering him as to surrendering him without compensation. It was all one to him, then and later, whether he supported Henry in a reconquest of England or surrendered Henry to the present conquerors of England, so only that the rulers of England supported his own battle against the central government of France. Edward, or his ambassadors, assured the Duke that the King had it in mind to marry Henry to his own daughter Elizabeth. The Duke allowed himself to be persuaded, and imagined his own best prospects to lie in handing over his guest to the union. Henry was passed to the ambassadors; he had fallen, they say, "through agony of mind, into a fever." It is not unlikely; his reluctance to return and his disbelief in the marriage were equally strong; he knew the daggers that had stabbed King Henry and Prince Edward, or the axe that had despatched his grandfather, would not be slow to end him if the King chose. The envoys, guarding the fabulous and feverish bridegroom, had reached St. Malo when they were overtaken. The Duke had changed his mind; he would not let Henry go. It may be he had become doubtful of the King's meaning and had a sense of decency towards his guest; it may be that he had determined to have greater assurances of aid from England before he gave up his great hold on England. His treasurer, Peter Landolf, came riding into the town. He found the ambassadors; he explained that his errand was to recover Henry. The ambassadors protested; there was conversation. During the conversation the Breton soldiers who had accompanied the Treasurer got hold of Henry and carried off "that most innocent ympe" to sanctuary. The ambassadors protested more vehemently, but they could not do anything. They were compelled to compromise on Landolf's promise that Henry should either be kept in the sanctuary where "by their negligence," as Landolf rather unkindly said, he now was, or be held in a stricter custody by the Duke. At least Henry, as he was carried back, had been saved from whatever kind of marriage had awaited him in England.

Nothing more of violence threatened him during the reign of Edward IV. He remained

"THAT MOST INNOCENT YMPE" 13

under restraint, observing as far as he could the activities of Europe. The restraint was relaxed on the death of Edward and the usurpation of Richard III. Richard was crowned on 6th July 1483. On 26th August 1483 the Duke of Brittany sent the new King a letter. He wrote that he had been several times urged by the King of France to deliver to the said King the person of " the lord of Richmond his cousin." He went on to dilate on the strength of the King of France, which was indeed continually in his thoughts for other reasons than any concerning the lord of Richmond. He added that he might be compelled, because of that strength, " of necessity to deliver to the said King Louis the said lord of Richmond, and to do other things to which he would be very loth for the injury which he knows the said King Louis would or might inflict upon the said King and Kingdom of England."

Such a letter, sent within seven weeks of Richard's seizure of the Throne, was obviously a threat. It was accompanied by a suggestion that Richard should send four thousand English archers to Brittany to operate if necessary against France, and help to keep the Duke independent; in which case there was every possibility that the lord of Richmond might be kept under renewed restraint. Richard did not see his way to satisfy the Duke's desires. It chanced, therefore, that on 22nd November in the same year the Duke issued a warrant to allow his treasurer to deliver ten thousand crowns of gold " to our most dear and well-beloved cousin the Lord of Richmond without making any difficulty therein . . . notwithstanding whatsoever commands, orders, prohibitions, restrictions, or other things to the contrary."

The immediate cause of this grant was the changed situation in England. In 1482 Henry's mother's second husband, Henry Stafford, had died, and she had married again. Her third husband was Thomas, Lord Stanley, a great person both with Edward IV and Richard III. She had so far left her early Lancastrian connexion behind that she carried the Queen's train at King Richard's coronation, but she had not left either the Buckingham relationship or her Tudor son behind. The present Duke of Buckingham was a descendant of John of Gaunt's brother on the father's side; on the mother's, he also was of the Beauforts. The removal of any real sense of allegiance was opening, to any of the nobility who was remotely connected with the Blood Royal, a possibility of the Crown. Buckingham had helped to gain it for Richard; within a few weeks of the coronation he had taken umbrage, retired from the Court, and was considering striking for himself. It is said that he had forgotten the existence of Richmond until one day, when he was out riding, he met by chance Richmond's mother, and he saw her and her son as "both bulwark and portcullis" between him and "the majesty royal and getting of the crown." It was said also, much later, that the Duke knew he had in his possession a version of the Act legitimatizing the Beauforts in which the critical words saving the royal dignity were omitted, and that he had once intended to give the said writing to the future King, but the Duke said that "he would not have done so for ten thousand pounds." Whatever the cause, he determined to be a king-maker rather than a king. He had tried with Richard, and Richard had disappointed him; he would try it again with the young man of twenty-six over the water. He discussed the matter with one then in his custody, John Morton, Bishop of Ely. Morton was a Balliol man, and a canon lawyer, and very nearly a great man; the description of him, ten years later, remains to us in the pages of Sir Thomas More. He was in 1483 a man of just over sixty; he had been a Lancastrian until Tewkesbury, when he had made his submission to the ruling house and had been employed and preferred by Edward. He had been one of the negotiators of the King's treaty with Louis of France, and had become Bishop of Ely in 1479. But on the usurpation of Richard he had been arrested on some pretext of being concerned in conspiracy—certainly because he was suspected of too great loyalty to Edward's sons, the Princes in the Tower. He had been handed over to Buckingham's custody, and Buckingham had removed his distinguished ecclesiastical prisoner from the Tower to Brecknock Castle, where he could be kept more safely not only from the Lancastrians but from the King, and where he now came to talk to him.

The Duke was very angry, and consequently very repentant. He lamented to the Bishop his folly in the past, his support of the wild boar who now crouched on the Throne. The Bishop listened cautiously, but did not at first commit himself. "When he understood his just cause of hatred," he became convinced of the new convert's probity. He may have sighed for the hatred as a Bishop, but he took advantage of it as a Lancastrian. It was known that a marriage between Henry Tudor and King Edward's daughter had once been suggested, and the proposal was now more seriously revived under the influence of Henry's mother. Morton and Buckingham sent messengers to Elizabeth's mother, the Dowager Queen of Edward IV, and found that the Countess Margaret's messengers were there before them, urging the same plan.

The Queen Dowager was then in sanctuary at Westminster with Elizabeth her daughter; she had fled there to be safe from the new King. Her sons had been in the Tower; now they had disappeared. They had been the chief danger to

"THAT MOST INNOCENT YMPE" 17

the new King. She was contented to pay herself back and to pay the King out with a son-in-law, though she was not a person whose conspiracies could be very firmly relied on. But she was only asked to agree. The arrival of the double embassy convinced her; she agreed to the marriage. Messengers were sent over to Brittany to inform Henry Tudor of the plans and to arrange for a co-ordination of movements.

Henry found himself offered the Crown. The primary importance of the offer was that it came from what had been the other side. It was conditional, but the condition was not very onerous; marriages of convenience were common enough, and he could hardly have hoped for a better, nor indeed for one as good. He knew very well how faint was his real claim to the Throne, however his Lancastrian partisans might brag of it, and if he had known of the paper the Duke of Buckingham was hiding, he would not have thought that made the claim much stronger. He was never a rash crusader; he weighed his chances. But the chances were all on one side; on the other was the mere certainty of quiescence in the power of the Duke of Brittany. The Duke had seemed kind of late, and had even talked of marrying Henry to his daughter Anne, but if Richard of England proved to be firmly settled and were willing to stand with Brittany, that was not at all a likely marriage. So long as he kept his person safe he could not lose much. He determined to go, but to go cautiously. He accepted the proposal; he promised to marry Elizabeth; he made preparations. He was informed that the rebellions were to begin through the south of England on 18th October simultaneously; it was hoped he would land in Wales by then. On 12th October he put to sea; fifteen ships carrying five thousand men—hired soldiers—rode on the waters under the Red Rose.

A storm struck them. Henry saw his fleet dispersed and his plans deranged by the skies. He eventually reached the English coast, his own ship accompanied only by one other, and sailed along it westwards towards Plymouth. At Plymouth he hesitated about landing, but from some uncertainty on the shore he took alarm and gave up the attempt. It was the first military crisis of his career; the second, and last, was Bosworth. He was saved this time by intelligence, as the next time by cunning. The rebellion had already failed, and the King's troops were hunting it down. Kent had risen too soon; and King Richard had seized his chance. A price was already on Buckingham's head. He had set up his standard at Brecknock, but a storm swelled the Severn; he was unable to cross and join the rebels in Devonshire. His soldiers began to desert; he himself fled, and was betrayed by the man with whom he took shelter. He was seized and executed on 2nd November.

Buckingham's claim to the Throne may have been small, but, such as it was, it had vanished. All possible Yorkist claimants seemed to be disappearing one by one. The Princes in the Tower were gone; Richard's own son was soon to die, and he would have to name as heir his nephew, John de la Pole, Earl of Lincoln. The White Roses were falling from their bush; on the Red, Henry was the last. He landed in Normandy on 30th October; thence he came again to Brittany, by permission of the French Government—which makes the Duke of Brittany's earlier letter a little odd. He heard of the collapse of the rebellion, the death of Buckingham, and the royal action towards the rebels. There were many attainders, but the King had been gracious to Henry's mother, Margaret, and only handed her over (with all her property) to the custody of her husband Lord Stanley. Bishop Morton had crossed to the Low Countries before the rebellion began. "After the Duke was engaged, and thought the Bishop should have been his chief pilot in the tempest," said Bacon unkindly, "the Bishop was gotten into the cockle-boat, and fled over beyond seas." Other lords, gentlemen, and clerics came over to Brittany: the Marquis of Dorset, son of the Queen Dowager before her marriage with Edward; the Bishop of Salisbury, the Bishop of Exeter; a Bourchier, a Courtenay, a Poynings. Allegiance was coming less than ever to mean anything. "The more party," wrote a City chronicler, "of the gentlemen of England were so dismayed that they knew not which party to take but at all adventure." More and more the growing opposition to Richard (helped by the rumours of the murder of the Princes in the Tower) necessarily meant support for the Tudor. More and more the exile found himself surrounded by something like a Court. It was at this juncture that the Duke of Brittany sent him the ten thousand crowns.

It was then that Henry determined to act by himself, to have at last a conspiracy, an army, and an oath of his own. It was more to his taste than joining some other. He always preferred to be with himself in secret than with others in frankness; now, however, he was frankly himself; the crowns may have determined him, for he must always be on good terms with money. By the end of 1483 he promulgated state. He still accepted the idea of marrying Elizabeth, and he made use of this to declare himself. He was twenty-seven years old, tall and lean, fair-haired and fair-skinned, with a smiling amiable face—"especially in his communication." The amiable smile of communication was not perhaps entirely disinterested; in later years he did not keep, or did not trouble to keep, the smile. But he presented himself all graciousness now. In the Cathedral of Rennes, on Christmas Day, he heard mass and stood up to make oath that he would marry the Princess Elizabeth as soon as he had achieved the Crown. His assembled Court did homage to him as if he were already anointed and crowned. He ceremonially put himself at the head of the Opposition, that is, at the head of the baronial party of Peace, Retrenchment, and Reform. He was to mean exactly that, and the three words were to mean rather more than his aristocratic supporters knew.

There was one possible hindrance to the intended marriage. Richard was presently talking of marrying Elizabeth himself, niece of his though she was. The Queen Dowager, bored with sanctuary, had on the collapse of the rebellion left it and gone over to Richard, daughter and all. The King kept the Princess Elizabeth in his power, as he did the only son of his other brother Clarence, the only other heir of his family, the small Earl of Warwick. He made renewed efforts to extract from Brittany the young man who had sworn, though not in any passion of romantic love, that he would certainly become Elizabeth's husband — when he had become King. He promised the Duke all the titles and revenues of Richmond if the Duke would send over to him the man who had pretended to be Earl of Richmond and was now pretending to be more than an earl. He issued pardons, in order to lure the Earl's supporters; notably he tried to recover John Morton, who in Flanders was another rallying point of the Opposition. He raised troops against the threat of invasion. And finally he talked of marrying Elizabeth.

A good deal depended on the Duke of Brittany, who seemed now to think that more might be gained by supporting Henry than by surrendering him. The Duke, however, embarrassed the exiles by going out of his mind, and leaving his ministers to decide. They were less inclined to believe in the grand ceremony of Rennes and much more inclined to come to terms with Richard. In June 1484 a thousand English soldiers landed in Brittany; they were not as many as the four thousand asked for, but they made a force. Morton from Flanders sent a priest, Christopher Urswick, to Henry with urgent warnings to escape, if possible, to France. Henry communicated with the French Government secretly and received favourable answers. France also was keeping in with both sides—a treaty with Richard, a haven for Henry, and a free hand for herself with Brittany.

It was September 1484. The Tudor determined to make his escape—by now, so hostile had the Government grown, it was no less. The ministers did not intend to lose whatever mortgage on England the possession of his

"THAT MOST INNOCENT YMPE" 23

person supplied. Henry dispatched his uncle Jasper with some of his followers on an ostensible visit to the Duke; they were to cross privately into France. He bade the rest, some five hundred in all, remain in the town of Vannes where he then was. But he himself rode out one day with five servants, and as soon as they were at a distance slipped with one of them into a wood and changed clothes. Then he rode fast for the frontier. It had taken the Breton watchers less than an hour to discover that their treasured exile had fled, and the Breton horse came riding hard after him. He won the race; he crossed the frontier; he came safely to the Court of France. In the November of 1484 he was given three thousand livres towards his needs, and went with the Court to Paris.

The English nobles continued to join him. The Duke of Brittany, somewhat recovered, allowed his other followers to come to France after him. Henry showed special delight at the arrival of the Earl of Oxford, who had been a strong Lancastrian and had been kept by Richard in the Castle of Hammes near Calais. He persuaded its captain his jailor to abandon his lord, King Richard, and both of them, Lancastrian and Yorkist, came to do obeisance to the Pretender. It is true the Marquis of Dorset had been almost lured away from Henry back to Richard by the persuasions of his mother, the

Dowager Queen. He left Paris for England, but his absence was discovered, and he was overtaken, and re-persuaded to return. Such swaying fortunes suggested to Henry that the full time had come, and that he and his supporters in England must trust and test each other. The French talked of helping him, but their own crises held them; they did no more. He must take his chance fully, for now either England must fall to him or his supporters must fall away. He managed to borrow money. He came to Rouen, and at Harfleur began to gather ships. It had been the port at which Henry V, the predecessor (perhaps) though not the ancestor of Henry Tudor, had begun and ended his victorious campaign in France some eighty years before.

At this point the proposed union of the Roses was threatened by the proposal of the incestuous union between the White Roses themselves. Richard, like the superb and unscrupulous Renascence intelligence that he was, saw that to rob Henry of his intended bride would be to leave him, not with only half a hereditary claim but with no hereditary claim at all. His moral position as leader of the Opposition would be left, but the King hoped that that could not yet be called national. Elizabeth of York was direct Plantagenet on her father's side and more national than this descendant of Welsh and French, and (at best) bastard Plantagenet. The Tudor was sending over letters talking of his "lineal inheritance of the Crown." Richard's wife Anne, the once-betrothed of the murdered Edward of Wales, had died, less than a year after the death of her son and the King's. Poison was rumoured, as it always was. Richard proposed to unite to himself the undoubted lineal inheritor of his brother, the late King, having (as some men believed) removed by assassinations in the Tower her more lineal brothers. It was a typical Renascence proposal, as he was a typical Renascence "tyrant." His supporters, however, in an equally typical sudden English fit of morality, discouraged the idea. He was compelled to disown and abandon it, and to rely on his secret service, his fleet, his cavalry stations along the south coast, his own military capacity and courage, and the support of such of the great nobles as remained, the Duke of Norfolk, for instance, and (he hoped and doubted) Lord Stanley, who held Lancashire and Cheshire, and Stanley's brother Sir William, who held North Wales. Lord Stanley was married to the Tudor's mother, but that was no reason for distrusting him. He asked leave to withdraw to his northern estates; it was not an absolute reason for distrusting him. The King granted permission, but he retained Stanley's son, Lord Strange, in his own custody.

Henry Tudor, away at Rheims, heard of the proposed incest, and was "nipped at the very stomach." He was hungry to be able to assert that stronger hereditary claim; he saw the advantage of being national in the name of his future wife till he could afford, being royal in his own, to abandon all possession but his own. The great ceremonial at Rennes was being spoilt for his supporters, and so for him. There emerged in his mind that odd dream of a dim prehistoric title which the casual genealogies of the time and his own capacity for rationalizing romanticism into contemporary fact made possible for him— the dream of Cadwallader. He thought again of the Welsh. He proposed—seriously or not—to marry the sister of Sir Walter Herbert who had power in Wales, and another of whose sisters was married to the great Earl of Northumberland. He sent letters to Herbert and Northumberland, but the messengers were caught. However, Richard had by then abandoned his marriage proposals, and the Tudor let his own substitute fall.

It was, nevertheless, Wales in which he trusted as his base. He had strong hopes of Sir William Stanley in the north, and now he received news that the chief man in the south, one Rhys ap Thomas, would follow him. Ap Thomas at the same time was swearing to King Richard that the invader should only enter over his prostrate body. Such double insurance of the future has always been a habit of great personages in English history, from the lords who communicated with Harfleur in the fifteenth century to the lords who communicated with St. Germains in the eighteenth. It might, were there a present claimant to the Crown in France or Austria, be even to-day renewed, though the ancient names are vanishing, and the Crown is a shadow. The Tudor determined to risk all. On 1st August 1485 he set sail, having with him a mixed force of some two thousand men. He was fortunate enough to escape Richard's ships, and on Sunday, 7th August, he disembarked his men at Milford Haven.

The habit of that age still dictated the invocation of God. The Tudor and his army sang the psalm *Judica me, Deus,* "Judge me, O God, and plead my cause." Henry was always careful to muster in any crisis all possible forces. The army advanced, in the name of St. George, towards North Wales. Henry behaved as if he were already king, as if the ceremony of the previous Christmas had been an incoronation. He knighted various candidates; his letters went before him superscribed "By the King." The Welsh lords came in; Pembroke submitted; English supporters came in. King Richard marched from London and came to Nottingham. Norfolk joined him; Northumberland joined him; Northampton joined him. Stanley did not; in answer to the King's urgent summons, he said he was ill. The King extracted a half-admission of the falsity of this from Lord Strange, and new letters were sent threatening the execution of Strange. Stanley began to move south.

The Tudor, a train of Welsh myth streaming behind him, and proclamations of his rightful claim (definite in tone but undefined in detail) shot out in front of him, and almost as uncertain as his royal adversary of the intentions of the Stanleys, advanced into England. He passed Shrewsbury; he passed Stafford; he reached Newport. At Stafford Sir William Stanley had an interview. He had already allowed the invader to pass into England unopposed, and the King caused him to be proclaimed a traitor. But his brother lay still at Lichfield with five thousand men, and the King dared not provoke him to hostility by any violent act. The Tudor one night, following his army in the rear, lost it. When they rediscovered each other in the morning he explained he had been in touch with "secret allies."

Certainly Stanley was on the point of being an ally; whose, no one quite knew; perhaps not he himself. The chance of the English crown was locked in his mind. His relation with the invader might have been regarded as deciding the matter, had not relative slain relative so often

"THAT MOST INNOCENT YMPE" 29

through these years. His allegiance to the King might have been held to decide the matter, had allegiance—and therefore treachery—still meant anything. The armies came nearer. On Sunday, 21st August, the King camped with his army near the village of Bosworth; the White Rose flew over the white tusks of Richard's cognizance the boar. The Pretender came up opposite early on the Monday morning. The armies deployed, the King's being the better and twice the size of his opponent's French, Welsh, and English levies. But behind the Tudor lay Sir William Stanley and between both armies, to Henry's left, lay Lord Stanley. And even now no one knew what Lord Stanley was going to do. Henry sent a last appeal, and still no one quite knew.

The King and the Tudor made speeches denouncing their opponents and heartening their men. The Pretender's army advanced; the King's moved to meet it. The Plantagenet himself plunged magnificently into the battle, the Tudor more cautiously, or perhaps he was merely less marked. But his army, though more mixed, was more reliable. The various levies which had joined the King were half hearted; the Earl of Northumberland and his men hardly moved; at the crisis Lord Stanley, hearing that his son had been rescued, came in. He gave to England, in the first footfall of his horse, a ruler, a dynasty, the Reformation, an

Elizabeth; he gave her the Stuart dynasty, the Rebellion, and the Whig Revolution; also, the Whig tradition of history, and the doubtful thesis that the freedom and security of the upper and upper middle classes is the same thing as, or a better thing than, the freedom and security of the lower middle classes and of the poor. He and his brother flung their men into the battle, and won it. In two hours the whole affair was done.

The King, when he saw that all was lost, made a last fierce effort to find and kill the Pretender. It is said he had actually come to blows with him when he was overborne and struck down. His crown had fallen from his helmet; it was found and brought to the Tudor. His lords fell, fled, or surrendered. The body of the last Plantagenet, on that day of high summer, was despoiled of its armour, thrown, naked and wounded, over a horse, and taken off to Leicester, where (as was the custom) it was exposed to public view, and afterwards buried by the Grey Friars. Later on his supplanter built him a tomb, something in the manner that Henry V had established masses for Richard II.

The last Rose had fallen. A cautious foot advanced, crushing the coloured past, among the armed lords and the shouting soldiery, to the perpetual vigil of a secret reign. Henry addressed his men; he gave " devout orisons " to God.

It is almost the last thing we hear of his having said; from then his mind was speechless except for official papers and diplomatic letters. He was twenty-seven, and there was no one else to be King of England.

CHAPTER II

"Change of Worlds hath caused Change of Mind"

Sir Hugh Conway, 1503.

OR rather there was. Of the three Plantagenet brothers, Edward IV and his sons were dead; his daughter Elizabeth was alive. Richard III was dead and his son; his nephew, John de la Pole, Earl of Lincoln, was alive. George, Duke of Clarence, was dead; his son, Edward, Earl of Warwick, a boy of ten, was alive, and his daughter Margaret, a girl of twelve. There were others in indirect lines of descent from Edward III—John Bourchier, Earl of Essex, and Edward Stafford, Duke of Buckingham, son of the Duke whom Richard had executed. The claims of Buckingham and Essex were not perhaps very strong, but on any hereditary principle they were both stronger than the Tudor. They could both claim by, and only by, the female line; he could do nothing better, and the women through whom they claimed were nearer the direct line than his, nor had their families been directly barred, as had his, from the succession. But these claimants had no more direct and obvious an appeal than his; and altruistic rebellions by the rest of the nobles in their favour were unlikely. The really serious danger was the male child of Clarence. He with his cousin, the Princess Elizabeth, the heir of Edward, had been sent by Richard to a castle in Yorkshire, well out of the way. Directly after Bosworth, during the Pretender's two days' stay at Leicester, a body of men was sent north to seize their persons. They were both taken to London, the boy to be inserted in the Tower and his sister (who was now twenty years old) to join her mother, the Dowager Queen.

There was one other woman left, since Henry could not get at her, to maintain the name, insolence, and glory of the house of York. She was Margaret, sister of Edward IV, wife and now widow of Charles the Bold, and therefore now Dowager Duchess of Burgundy. She was a woman of thirty-nine, some ten years younger than the English Dowager, and she had not her sister-in-law's tendency to sway from side to side. She had, wrote Francis Bacon, "the spirit of a man and the malice of a woman"—though, to be sure, Bacon had never studied women, as may be seen by his essay on "Marriage"; it was almost his only omission, and permissible. She was then in the Low Countries, at Malines, settled among the cities which were to maintain for so long their tradition of independence—as long, through all changes of mode, as till yesterday when the King of the Belgians imposed his own foreign policy upon, if not against, the Powers. But at that time it was the cities, as cities, that counted. The religious quarrel had not yet begun ; there was no talk of Calvinist or Catholic. Yet the difficulties of the overlordship of the Netherlands were the same in any age.

It is perhaps largely to those cities, and especially to the histories of them which have been generally circulated among us, that we owe our idea that to throw off lordship, as such, is a good thing, and that independence, as such, is better than obedience. It is perhaps to the coloured spectacle of their undoubted heroism that we owe the vague notion that a man cannot find freedom by continuously choosing to obey. Out of which idea, by a process of reaction and conversion, arise Fascisms, dominations, and all mortal totalitarian powers. Among those yet unshaped liberties, and among the growing clamour of their shaping, Margaret of Burgundy maintained belief in the Hereditary Kingship of England, and provided shelter and support for any enemy of the house of Lancaster, and especially of its still more obscure and base offshoot, the house of Tudor.

The Pretender had one immediate business— to make it clear to everyone that he was already the King. He must not be King by descent, or by betrothal, or even by victory, or by any cause, for all causes would raise objections and create schisms. The fact must be accepted merely as a fact; it must not be rationalized or explained. This, the single point at which he had been aiming since he made up his mind to develop his own conspiracy, must be the single point upon which the future of England was to rest. He reproduced it in every word and every action; because so many arguments were possible he could permit no argument. He who all his life foresaw and provided for alternatives could not here allow any alternative. He was immediately and universally exclusive, and he proceeded to advance gently to London and to the exhibition of his uniqueness.

He reached it on Saturday, 27th August. At the Rise of Hornsey the Lord Mayor, Thomas Hyll, the Aldermen, and the crafts, clothed in violet, came to meet him, and he and his civic train passed on to St. Paul's. The reception was habitual enough; less than a year before they had gone out similarly to meet Richard, who was returning to the city. But now, more than ever before, it was the meeting of allies—allies of whom one was to direct and one to be directed, but still allies. The merchants and capitalist powers of the city met a king who understood the value of capitalism and merchandise. It was not then possible for the Kingship to be quite so domestic as it has since become, and certainly

Henry, though he never offended against, never exhibited more than, a courteous domesticity. But if he was not suburban at home he was almost suburban at work. He "went up to the city" every day of his life, if not literally, at least metaphorically. He had in him a good deal of a careful Chairman of a limited liability company. He disliked speculation. He had had to speculate in the raid on England, and he had made his profit at Bosworth. Now he rode into London, surrounded by the other directors of that national company of which, by Bosworth's lucky and bloody chance, he had become Chairman, and he took up the tasks that were to engage him all his life: the alteration of the personnel of the Board, the strengthening of the Chairman's position, the alteration of the medium in which the Company dealt—white metal for red, silver for steel. Plantagenet was down and Tudor was up. Hardly any Tudor cared to take a chance—except perhaps Mary, and she in religion where she knew it for her duty, nor there did she suppose it to be a chance, as indeed at that time it hardly was.

They reached St. Paul's. The standards of the Pretender were to be offered at the High Altar. They were a curious group—the arms of Edward III enriched by Tudor Roses; the cross of St. George; the Red Dragon of the old kings of Wales; and a banner bearing a dun cow on a yellow field. No one seems to have recorded what this meant. Around the dun cow thanksgivings were offered; the *Te Deum* sung; God, the Mother of God, angels and archangels, saints and confessors, invoked. Henry went home with the Bishop of London; the citizens dispersed. It is, strictly, irrelevant, but it has always struck the fancy of historians that another visitor followed Henry—the Sweating Sickness. Within a month the Lord Mayor who welcomed him was dead; five of the aldermen perished, and " many worshipful commoners." Another mayor was chosen immediately; in four days he, too, had died. A kind of superstition was felt in the air; men shuddered at the omen of a " sweating reign."

Meanwhile the dun cow put on its glory. The Tudor exhibited himself as King. He took no immediate steps about the marriage to Elizabeth. Instead of a wife he gave himself a bodyguard; a thing new to English kings, borrowed from the custom of the kings of France. It served for safety, for splendour, for the more awful aloofness of his person; it was the certainty and fact of the King. He became royal in his dress and surroundings, beginning that habit of gorgeousness which, for all his economy, he continued to maintain. There he carried on and converted the virtue of the Middle Ages into the indulgence of the Renascence, as so many did.

The difference between the medieval and Renascence ages was often not so much in act as in the manner of the act. Henry VII is the alteration of the manner, in every sense. " It has often been disputed whether the reign of Henry VII belongs to the Middle Ages or to the Renascence. From the point of view of the numismatist the answer is quite clear—the early years of the first Tudor king were distinctly medieval. But equally clearly his last issues are pure Renascence. . . . And Henry was a great innovator, as witness the two boons which he gave to the currency—the gold sovereign and the silver shilling." [1]

It was, in Mr. Oman's symbolical sentences, the gold sovereign with which Henry was first chiefly concerned, though he never forgot the silver shilling, or the number of shillings that went to make up the sovereign. He had his friends and his enemies to deal with. He scattered a few titles: his uncle Jasper became Duke of Bedford; Thomas, Lord Stanley, became Earl of Derby; Sir Edward Courtenay, who had been with him in Brittany, became Earl of Devon; Edward Stafford, a boy of seven, son of the executed Duke of Buckingham, was restored to the Duchy. On the whole, however, he took care not to create, nor to seem to create, a new nobility. He himself— it was the very root of the myth he now set out to create—was not new but very old; as old as

[1] *The Coinage of England*, C. Oman, Clarendon Press.

Cadwallader, or at least as Plantagenet, much older in his natural descent than in his accidental, either as the son of the legitimatized son of the lover of the French widow of Henry V, or as the descendant of the legitimatized bastards of the mistress and later wife of John of Gaunt. He did not desire to make a crowd of new nobilities. His friends had done no more than their duty. As for his enemies, he was prepared to forgive them on condition that they left off being his enemies. Such behaviour certainly was less than Christian, but it agreed with the general level of Henry's piety. This was real enough; he had a concern for his salvation. He founded at that time a chantry for himself, his mother, and his forefathers. The accident that mingled the later Tudors with the Reformation controversies has made it easy to think vaguely of Henry as half-Reformation already. But in fact it was not so. He existed before those controversies, in the full habit of the medieval Church, however corrupt in certain high places that Church had become. What can be known of him, therefore, must be known in that relationship; even his hypocrisy, if any, his superstition, his devotion.

It is likely therefore that his moderation towards his enemies was affected by his religion, though to demand the conversion of enemies before forgiving them is precisely less than Christian. Nor did he hasten even with that modified pardon. He was still intent on the fact of himself as King. He determined his Coronation for 30th October; he sent out writs for a Parliament to meet on 7th November. He would be formal as well as actual King before Parliament met. Nothing was to depend on Parliament except ratification of the *status quo* and money; and even money presently was not to depend on Parliament.

About him at Westminster on that October day were his friends and servants, his relations and supporters: all clients, no confidants. The Duke of Bedford carried the Crown; the Earl of Derby, the sword; John de la Pole, Duke of Suffolk (who had married King Richard's sister and was the father of King Richard's heir), the sceptre; Henry Bourchier, Earl of Essex, the spurs. John Morton was back as Bishop of Ely; another priestly and diplomatic servant, Richard Fox, was Bishop of Exeter. Henry rode on a horse caparisoned with cloth of gold, in a long gown of " purpure velvet," furred with ermine, laced with gold, tasselled with gold; over him a golden canopy. He rode alone; there was no favourite, no wife, no child. He was anointed and crowned.

In such a formal stability he met the Parliament. He was very wise; things might have been said or done against a claimant to royalty which were impossible against the anointed image of royalty. The Lords and Commons found, however, that they were expected to do more than accept; they were meant to assert. The Lords were few in number: some thirty spiritual peers, and some seventeen lay. The reason was that not only were all the strong Yorkists naturally absent, but so were many strong Lancastrians. They had been attainted under Richard, and their attainders were yet unreversed. They were therefore "out of law" and incapable of sitting. The judges had been consulted and they had so decided. It is true that the King himself was under the same incapacity; he had been attainted by Edward IV and was still technically an outlaw. This point was put to the judges. They answered that the mere fact that he had taken on himself the supreme authority freed him, *ipso facto*, from the taint. The argument ran roughly: could any outlaw be king? No; but King Henry was king; therefore he was not outlaw. It was clear that the lawyers at any rate had accepted the King's single dogma. He proceeded to have it defined—for themselves—by the Parliament.

It was opened by a sermon, in which the King was likened by Morton, who was made Lord Chancellor, to Joshua (though he did not pursue the comparison so far as to see in Lord Stanley a type of Rahab the harlot). The King made the members a speech on the customary subject of his just inheritance, especially as proved by the Justice of God at Bosworth, and on the peace and protection which all who did not offend him should enjoy. It was the turn of the members to reply, and the terms of their reply were certainly shaped by the King. Their declaration did not touch causes, nor did it in any way provide the King with his kingdom. It professed that "in avoiding of all ambiguities and questions . . . the inheritance of the Crowns of England and France . . . be rest, remain, and abide in the most royal person of our new sovereign lord King Henry the Seventh, and in the heirs of his body lawfully coming, perpetually with the grace of God so to endure and in none other."

It was a victory for the King almost as remarkable as Bosworth. It would throw a great deal of light on the nature of Henry and on the nature of his methods if we knew how the thing was worked. In one way, indeed, it was obvious. Richard was dead; the nearest male heir was a minor; the proper female heir was to be (it was understood) Henry's wife; peace and unity were urgent. It is not very surprising that they should have accepted the Tudor. But how did it come about that they accepted him so? Did anyone of them desire to put a reason in the declaration, and how was he persuaded to leave it out? How far did Henry admit to himself or to others the necessity of leaving reasons out? How far did he know what he was and how far did he believe himself what he was not? How far did the old myth of Cadwallader work within him? did he despise as modern upstarts the very men to whom he must himself seem something of an upstart? What, at that point of his life, were his private conversations with his servants?

It is the lack of all such knowledge throughout his reign that leaves Henry to us indeed as a king without a face. There are no memoirs nor correspondence in which he appears, even by chance, in daylight and in action. He had his servants, the group of peers and priests and gentlemen who carried out his intentions. He had, that is to say, his instruments. In their lives they were content to remain instruments; it was his good fortune. Morton never became as decisive as Wolsey nor Fox as argumentative as Cecil. After their deaths they remained loyal, and no word escaped from their tombs to betray to future ages the heart of a king. Their silence covered his own tomb with stone; peeping and botanizing there is impossible. One can only examine a few cracks.

Certainly the declaration demanded as little as possible from its supporters; it left everyone free to think what they liked about the Pretender's claims so long as they admitted the King's existence. But it suggests also the King's self-restraint that he should have been capable of

permitting that and of demanding only that.
Attempting no title where he could show no title,
he did what few can do; he refrained from
provoking opposition by the effort of disproving
it. The restraint made the single demand more
emphatic, leaving no loophole for modification
or argument. The single engine stood ready to
strike once and strike no more.

He imposed it upon them. They were, on the
whole, his friends; they were not unwilling to
have him. He proceeded to impose more difficult
things, for though they were his friends they were
still of one general kind, and he had lately been
of that kind. He had been Earl of Richmond,
and they all knew that if he were now anything
more it was due to them, to Lord Stanley, and the
luck of Bosworth. In spite of that, he compelled
them to treat their new declaration seriously;
he compelled them to recognize the Crown in four
separate Acts. The word at that moment
conveys rather more than it does in our contemporary colloquialisms. These Acts were acts
indeed; the lords, clergy, and gentlemen of that
Parliament did something. They created the
prestige and power of the King almost before the
King himself existed.

The first Act concerned property. They
restored to the Crown all lands alienated from
the Crown for thirty years—since 2nd October
1455, excepting only those granted since the

beginning of the present reign. In 1455 the civil war had hardly begun; the first skirmish had happened at St. Albans in May, and that was all. There was no effort at general restoration, nor could there be; the seizures, confiscations, attainders, and murders had been too many. It does not seem that Henry entered upon any general campaign of resumption of land. What he gained was the title to do it; he caused to be thrown open to him the possibility of thrusting any property-owner who had, in the course of those thirty years, come to possess any land originally the Crown's into a maze of legal complication. It might give any landowner—and may have given most—urgent reasons for "keeping in" with the King. It threw over all the property of the Board of Directors (so far as they were landholders) a dim legal claim of the Chairman's. Probably, as long as they were all good friends, the Chairman would do nothing; perhaps he would not gain much if he did. But he might cause a maximum of inconvenience to his opponents—even, in the end, to the striking of the single engine.[1]

The second Act was more usual at such a time. It was the passing of the new attainders: of Richard, of the Duke of Norfolk and his son the

---

[1] In 1495 a further Act restored, officially, to the Crown all land alienated since "Edward III and Richard II." It did not happen, but it was always a possibility.

Earl of Surrey, and some twenty-three other gentlemen, dead or alive, who had fought for Richard. What was remarkable in it was the date which delimited attainder. The reign was officially declared to have begun before Bosworth, so that anyone who fought against Henry at Bosworth, or indeed anyone who had not supported Henry at Bosworth, was technically guilty of treason. Richard III was accused (as well as of " shedding infants' blood ") of assembling an army for the traitorous destruction of the King's royal person. Certainly King Richard had had every intention of destroying the person of the then Pretender. But it had never occurred to anyone that the effort of even a usurping Plantagenet against an untitled Tudor could be described as treachery and rebellion. Everyone knew that Henry's royalty had not in fact begun till, at earliest, the end of Bosworth on 22nd August. The new Act assumed that it had begun certainly on that 21st August " in the first year of the reign."

Either morality, or anxiety about the precedent now set for any future Pretender to demand support on peril of death or attainder, caused the lords to demur. " There were many gentlemen against it." It was forced through—perhaps the most surprising exhibition of the power which Henry already felt himself capable of exercising. It was his decision ; the rest yielded.

The third Act was not so much a law as an oath, and was again unpopular. On 19th December the King came in person to the Parliament. In a full gathering the proceedings began by the administration of the oath to the gentlemen of the Household. The Commons followed; lastly, the Lords submitted themselves—thirty spiritual and eighteen lay peers. It was an oath for the peace of the land by the reform of certain evils, and all swore to the reform. They swore not to entertain in their service any offenders against the law, not to swear men to their own personal service, or to give "livery, sign, or token contrary to law," not to take any action against the King's writs, not (in short), to make of themselves, separately or together, any nucleus of established power in separation from or disobedience to the Crown. They might administer; they were not to rule. They might enjoy fidelity; they must not—as against the law—demand loyalty. "The law" meant the King. There were to be no more great households of almost sovereign extent and number; no more outbreaks or demonstrations in arms; no more violent bands careless of any will but their immediate master's. Or at least everyone should swear faith against it. One after another all the King's servants, personal and national, laying their right hands on the book of the Gospels, took the oath.

The fourth Act was a petition. After Henry had reached London he had renewed to the gentlemen he had summoned to him his promise to marry Elizabeth of York. Since then he had shown no haste to proceed with the marriage. He would not permit any talk of Elizabeth's title to the Crown, even as coming in aid of his. He would have no aid to what was his own; he would not have her mentioned in the Declaration of Allegiance. Allegiance must be his absolutely. But, that understood, he was perfectly willing to keep the oath of Rennes. Only he was determined to get all he could out of it. He would keep his vows and see to it that his vows kept him, in this world as in the other. He caused therefore a request to be addressed to him by the whole Parliament on 10th December, when he had come down to prorogue it, that he should marry the Princess Elizabeth of York. The Commons presented it; the Lords rose in support. The old oath of Rennes was not mentioned; the King was entreated to quieten, satisfy, and delight his subjects. The King was pleased to consent. In this again he had freed himself from dependence. The oath of Rennes remained a fact, but it was a Henrician policy to fulfil it as a convenience to and at the request of others rather than as a personal duty. He gave to the Crown therefore an even greater prestige of aloofness. It existed unconditioned by the past of its wearer; it consented, but it was not constrained.

The Declaration and the four Acts that accompanied it were a sufficiently remarkable achievement for those five weeks. They became the bodyguard of the idea of the King, as his actual bodyguard of his person. So far as words could do it, words formed into laws, oaths, and petitions, the Pretender had established not only his occupation but his unique occupation of the Throne. He was King by the declaration; by the first Act, all landed property that had been his predecessors' might be justly recovered to his Kingship, save such as he might himself have given away; by the second, he had always had his Kingship, in spite of treasonable rebellions by the late Duke of Gloucester; by the third, all right of civil obedience belonged to his Kingship alone, and all contrary interpretation had been solemnly forsworn; by the fourth, the Kingship consented to the petitionary appeals of his subjects to raise into itself the representative of a lesser, an unroyal, house. In all these ways the Kingship rose and remained unique.

It was probably Henry's own chief doing. But it may not have been unassisted by a particular group of his instruments. The Lords in that Parliament, it will be remarked, consisted of nearly twice as many spiritual peers as of lay—thirty to eighteen. Ecclesiastical influence therefore stood high, and one of the chief ecclesiastics, in relation with the King, in power and influence, if not in rank, was John Morton, Bishop of Ely. Morton was a man of sixty; he was a man who took his religion seriously. There is little sign that he dominated or influenced the King. But he was a Bishop as well as the King's servant, and perhaps he was the King's servant because he was a Bishop. He had been a Lancastrian till Edward IV was King; he had submitted to Edward because he was King; he had been at least inimical to the illegal seizure of the Crown by Richard; he had supported the opposition to Richard, once the opposition was declared and certain, because he planned to unite the warring Houses in peace. He desired peace.

It was, after all, the business of the Bishops —or, at least, subject to greater concerns, it was the business of the Bishops—to pursue peace. In the general suspicion engendered by history it is possible to underrate the extent to which the Bishops then, as at other times, took their duties seriously. The influence of the hierarchy of the Church was on the side of union and peace, and on the side therefore of a strong monarchy as making for union and peace. It may be argued, certainly, that the Bishops had, by the nature of things, that semi-independence which the lay lords were attempting to gain by livery and maintenance, by their indentured ruffians and resistance to the King's writs. If that was so, it yet remains true that they did not encourage the lay lords to emulate individually and without principle what they themselves maintained as a principle and corporately. They stood for the King, and what Morton had spoken secretly to Buckingham in Brecknock was now declared openly by his fellows. The King's piety encouraged them, as their support encouraged his promulgation of himself, and all over England the resources of the Church were at his devout disposal in favour of himself, because he himself meant peace.

Nor did the ecclesiastical help end there. The King determined to canopy the dragon throne of Cadwallader, now established and bushed between the White Roses and the Red, with a cloud of Roman sanctions. His peace and his reign were to be confirmed by the sentence of supreme spiritual jurisdiction. He applied to Rome for two instruments, and he gained both. A Bull of the Roman See, issued in the next March, proclaimed all rebels against Henry *ipso facto* excommunicate. Henry was pontifically declared King (i) by victory, (ii) by succession, (iii) by choice and vote of all the realm and of the three estates. He was King in every way and on every ground. "The accumulation of reasons," said Bishop Stubbs, "may show that Innocent VIII had some misgivings." The story of the lonely boy who thus gathered thunder to his support ought to be one of the more romantic tales of history. But Henry's diplomatic capacity and Henry's refusal to expand into any spectacular moments make it read like a series of normal business transactions. The Bull had, perhaps, one result on the future; it accentuated the tendency of rebels to become or to produce Pretenders. Rebels were *ipso facto* excommunicate. But a dispossessed true monarch was, *ipso facto*, not a rebel, nor were his supporters. It was desirable therefore that any military operation against Henry should be made under the title of a royal claim, and in fact most were.

The second Papal instrument was a dispensation for the marriage of Henry and Elizabeth, and this also was not without its effect on the future. Henry, having sent in the application, was quicker to concede his marriage to his petitioners than he had been to celebrate it for himself. The Legate resident in England issued a temporary dispensation, and the marriage was celebrated on the 18th January 1485/6. On 6th March the Holy See confirmed the Legate's action. Such a method, natural enough in such a case, encouraged faintly the idea that in marriage affairs ecclesiastical action taken by the Legate would be confirmed by the tardier operation of Rome—an idea rooted in the mind of Henry's son, who, in his own matrimonial dilemma, quite obviously and sincerely imagined himself to have been cheated by the Holy See.

The marriage took place. Elizabeth, however, received no public coronation for almost two years; she had to wait until 25th November 1487. Henry could restrain himself even better on behalf of other people than on his own. In the long interval two things had happened; the Simnel revolt on behalf of York had been crushed and an heir had been born. As a consequence the coronation appears as an ostentation of the security of a King who was about to become a dynasty. It was almost an acknowledgment of the current feudal service, or contract, of the King's wife. She was brought by water from Greenwich to the Tower where the greatness of her husband received her in a " joyous and comfortable " manner. She went by land from the Tower to Westminster where, after the coronation, she was feasted under the eyes of the King and his mother, the Lady Margaret, who watched from a balcony. She continued her feudal service for some years afterwards.

The birth of the heir was carefully arranged to take place at Winchester. In the summer of 1486 the King left London to hunt in the New Forest. He reached Winchester in September, and there the Queen was brought. A male child was born on 20th September. He was christened Arthur. In the reign of another Henry—the second—the reputed tomb of Arthur at Glastonbury, not so far from Winchester, had been opened and the bones of a man of more than ordinary size discovered there. In the time of the seventh Henry the reputed Round Table of that ancient Arthur hung in the Cathedral; it bears now the painted Roses of the two Houses. Winchester was thus doubly related to the great ancestor, and the new prince was born in the midst of those myths and tales. The peculiar Welsh claims of Cadwallader were fused with the more English and even European claims of Arthur. The dynasty was to be no more Welsh than it was to be Lancastrian or Yorkist. It was to have a claim that could rank with the proudest of France or Spain; the Valois himself could not boast of better blood than that which flowed in the hero of the Matter of Britain and in his descendants Henry King of England and Arthur Prince of Wales (he was made so in November 1490). How far Louis or Ferdinand believed it was of no importance; there is no reason to suppose they did not, and in any case it removed a possible inconvenience and exhibited the King as belonging fully to the guild of his royal fellows.

The births of the other children followed at intervals: in 1489 Margaret, in 1491 Henry, in 1496 Mary. There was also the little Prince Edmund, who lived only a year. Had it been

"CHANGE OF WORLDS" 55

the custom then to issue reproductions of paintings of the Royal Family (and it is to be feared Henry would have approved, but he would have approved for a purpose and with an intention, not helplessly), the group of the King and Queen with their children would have contained for us now two centuries of English history. There in 1496 would have been the most negligible of all, the baby princess, in her mother's arms. There, standing on the left of his seated father, would have been the Prince Arthur, to be betrothed next year to the Spanish Princess Katherine, and four years later to be married and to die, leaving in his widow the most dangerous, perhaps in some ways the most disastrous, legacy that ever a Prince of Wales gave to his country. There before the King would have been the five-year-old Henry, holding the hand of his seven-year-old sister Margaret. The shadow of that Spanish princess whom the painting did not include by a year touched him, and within her shadow the ghosts of the dead children she was to bear him, and of the Carthusians and the rest of the executed martyrs, and about his feet the spirits of his children who were to be—Edward, and another Mary, and Elizabeth, most like her grandfather. But Henry's older sister Margaret would have been handing the spirits at her feet the images of twofold balls and treble sceptres, through her unseen husband the King of Scotland

—to yet a third Mary and to James and to Charles and another Charles and another James, and the spirits playing with the crowns would have broken them like the apes in *Faust*; and deep in the foreground would have lain, like monstrous shapes that were oppressed by the King's sceptre stretched out over them, but already themselves stretching out their own hands towards those unborn and unconscious spirits, as if to grasp the golden playthings— the shapes of the Families. The chamber in which that group was taken would have been the Star Chamber, the room of the King's own Court, and through the windows of it the fields would have been white with sheep, and beyond the sheep the sea and the shapes of the vessels in which at different times the defeated English Kings were to fly from the Families and from the English people to whom, occasionally, those Kings tried to be true. The Wars of the Roses were over, and for two centuries the roses, white and red alike, were to thrive in the great gardens of manors and other huge houses where, for good or for evil, the Families would build themselves over England and order royalty, like the roses, at their will. But the eyes of the man who had been so lately Pretender and was now the King would not see the shapes, nor the sheep, nor the ships, because they would be turned towards the solemn serious figure approaching the group from without, the unseen daughter of Ferdinand and Isabella, the Princess of Spain and the Indies and Jerusalem, kingdoms as real as Henry's own or as mythical as the fabulous Arthurian royalty his diplomacy and his superstition were endeavouring to revive.

CHAPTER III

THE KING AND THE KINGS

THE future history of Henry divides itself, in subject, into the wars, at home and abroad, that he did not want, and the marriages and commerce that he did; in time, into the period 1485-99 when he was in control of his policy, and the period 1499-1509 when his policy began to get control of him. At the moment when he became safe he grew old. "The King has aged by twenty years," wrote the Spanish ambassador in 1499. He watched vigilantly all his life till then; it seemed, then, as if something had abandoned him to his occupation. He had certainly enough to watch; he who had successfully asserted a doubtful claim to the Throne was to be harried, all that first period, by doubtful claims to the Throne. He is always listening to the wind in the arras and under the door; it must be admitted that the noise of the wind never fretted him into distraction from his game of diplomatic chess.

He fought his rivals down. Yet he did not much care for war. He had won his kingdom by arms, but he did not believe in arms. He knew that only the firmest determination and the strictest policy could carry arms to a successful conclusion, and he conceived that that policy and determination might succeed without arms. Besides, this recourse to arms, for him who was no great military genius, involved a high element of chance, and he did not care to depend on chance. Bosworth had depended, much more than he could approve, on the chance of Lord Stanley. Henry did not desire to depend on any Stanley, at home or abroad, or on anyone in the rôle of Stanley. He wished, as far as possible, to eradicate chance by being prepared for all chances. His instructions to his envoys—to Fox and Urswick and Richard Edgcumbe and the rest —are always remarkable for their continued alternatives. They arrange against any possible variation. There is a chance in all things, but in war more than most; in commerce, on the whole, less. Henry preferred to reply on the slower, quieter, and securer method—by his temperament, by his experience, but also by his intellect. Wool instead of weapons; trade instead of trumpets; the glory of gold instead of the less reliable gold of glory. " He coveted to accumulate treasure," wrote Bacon, " and was a little poor in admiring riches." Bacon was not blaming the King there for a wrong policy; it was the mind behind the policy he criticized, the admiration of riches, not merely their accumulation.

But Bacon's criticism was that of a mind possessed of an impulse of interior magnificence. His own care was for riches only for the sake of his august gospel of learning; he was never pernickety. Henry Tudor lacked the nobler impulse; his exterior magnificence, which was great, was dictated not apparently by love but by policy. There is a sad story told by the Papal Envoy in 1489: "We have opened the money-box which the King was pleased to have at his court; we found in it £11, 11s., which result made our hearts sink within us; for there were present—the King, the Queen, the mother of the King, and the mother of the Queen, besides dukes, earls, and marquises, and other lords and ambassadors, so that we expected to have much more." This was not Henry's economy alone, but it serves to exemplify that economy.

He was provident by nature and by intellect, and the same caution that dictated a show of royalty in dress and carriage decreed an evasion of battle and of the chance of defeat or death. But it is only fair to stress the point that his judgment of his problems coincided with the habit of his being; his circumstances turned what might have been vices into something like virtues, though they lacked the greatness of their kind and the grand scope of sanctity. He was determined upon the medium and manner in which his campaigns should be fought; in that sense he may be said to have imposed his will before the battle and even to have prevented the battle.

But he could not altogether prevent it. Bosworth had not been generally accepted in the north, where the city of York itself declared its grief at the result and was at odds with the new King over the choice of a new Recorder. Henry was content partly to yield to the city and partly to overawe it by ostentatiously displaying before them the actual fact. At the beginning of March 1485–86 he set out on one of those royal progresses which were a feature of his reign. He took with him a great company of the peers who had declared him to be King. There were, however, still alive and in hiding, but in action too, certain peers and gentlemen who had not, and they were raising the country before and against him. As he moved north, hostility spasmodically awoke. " The King," said Bacon, " thought it was but a rag or remnant of Bosworth . . . but he was more doubtful of the raising of forces to resist the rebels.' At Nottingham he heard that Yorkshire was in arms, that York was threatened by one body of rebels and Worcester by another. Lord Lovell led the one and Sir Humphrey Stafford with his brother Thomas the other. But before there was any clash the prestige and proclamations of the King dissolved the armies. " His manner was to send his pardons rather before the sword than after," and they succeeded. Lovell disappeared, and managed to get oversea to the Dowager Duchess of Burgundy; the Staffords fled to sanctuary. Sanctuary was losing its power of protection. Judges were asked whether sanctuary might shield traitors; they decided that it could not. The lawyers supported the Crown, and the clergy were no longer anxious to pursue the dispute. The Staffords were taken from refuge and put to trial. The King passed on to York and found a converted city pealing loyalty. It presented a great splendour of reception. Pageants of the most famous personages of Biblical and Christian tradition implored the royal benignity. "At the wider end of House Brigge" King Solomon made a speech, appearing in order to do so in the midst of a show of Henry's landing at Milford Haven. He submitted his own wisdom to Henry's, for (he said) he had revolved

"How with sapience ye have spent your space
To the time of this your reign mysteriously."

The adverb defines a general feeling. The King had come as a mystery, "out of the everywhere into here." There were parts of England where it could not have very well been known who or what he was, only what he was not. He was not anyone expected. He knew it; he knew it remained to show them everywhere the fact of himself and he proceeded to do so.

Another pageant " of the Assumption of our Lady " caused the Blessed Virgin to assure the King that

> " this City is a place of my pleasing,
> Then have thou no dread nor no doubting."

At the other end of the same street King David submitted his sword of victory, and also interceded for the city which he had chosen for his place, having while he reigned in Juda (so he said) heard of its founding by Ebronius. Verse was still free from anachronism, as painting was from perspective—those good discoveries which were later on so overdone. Moved by these heavenly appeals, the King excused the city from making him the usual present of money, and became even more popular. On his way back to London he was met by our Lady once more at Hertford. There she welcomed him as her own true knight, and exhorted him to keep himself free " from all fraudulent imagination " —a good phrase, and a good piece of advice for Henry, who all his life was compelled to have frequent dealings with the " fraudulent imagination," both others' and his own.

The very next year indeed saw such an imagination in action. There is in the whole of English history no story of a Pretender so closely followed by false pretenders. Several things conspired to encourage them. There were the tales of the killing of the Princes in the Tower under Richard which provided the possibility of fraudulent princes; there was the Pope's Bull, which made them desirable. They began to exist; how we do not know, nor with what details of mystery the first was prepared. A certain priest of Oxford, named Richard Symons, dreamed of tutoring a king, and in one of his pupils saw the king he dreamed he was tutoring. His imagination became fraudulent. He fled with his pupil to Ireland. The pupil, whose name was Lambert Simnel, was presented to the Irish lords as the young Earl of Warwick who had (it was declared) escaped from the Tower. The Irish accepted him joyously. News of him went to Flanders and to England—to King Henry in his palace at Sheen. He saw himself confronted with a threat against which his legal and his matrimonial actions had been directed, the appearance of a claimant to royalty. He countered it by producing the actual Earl of Warwick from the Tower and parading him through London. Stringent measures, surprisingly, were taken against the Dowager Queen, Elizabeth's mother, who had perhaps drifted into this conspiracy as easily as she had drifted out of others. If so, Henry determined that her resources should not drift with her. He confiscated her property, and gave it to her daughter and his wife, Elizabeth. He relegated her to a convent, there to plot if she could. She never had done—not anything that could be called *plotting* : she was very different from his own mother Margaret and from the Dowager Duchess of Burgundy. She was not badly treated, but she was suppressed. It removed another potential source of danger ; there was to be no chance of a domestic recognition of the new Pretender by an old woman who might care for Henry no more than she had cared for Richard. The act was followed a month or two later by the arrest and imprisonment of her son the Marquis of Dorset, who had been with the King (and had left the King) in France. At the same time a general pardon was issued to all those—however traitorous—who now submitted to the King.

There had been at the Council when some of these measures were settled John de la Pole, Earl of Lincoln, whom Richard III had proclaimed his heir. He, having taken part in the Council, went off and presently escaped, following Lovell to the Court of the Duchess. There was a threat from Ireland in the west and from Flanders in the east, and the shores had to be manned against invasion as they had been under Richard III. The King went to the great shrine of Our Lady of Walsingham as an act of devotion, and caused the Papal Bull in his favour to be read publicly. Excommunication was denounced against all rebels. It may have been partly in an attempt to avoid this ecclesiastical censure that Lincoln and Lovell determined to support the fraudulence of the pretended Earl of Warwick in Ireland. Three weeks after they had reached Ireland Simnel was crowned in Dublin as Edward VI, and eleven days later he and his whole force of Irish kerns, German mercenaries, and the households of English gentlemen descended upon Lancashire. The King was then in middle England, and made preparations to move against them. Both sides were anxious not to outrage the common people. The leaders of the revolt took care that as little injury as possible should be done to the inhabitants. Henry issued almost a complete code of behaviour for armies in the field.

" The King our Sovereign Lord straitly charges and commands that no manner of man, of whatsoever state, degree, or condition he be, rob nor spoil any church, nor take out of the same any ornament therein belonging, nor touch nor set hand on the pyx wherein the Blessed Sacrament is contained ; nor yet rob nor spoil any manner man or woman, upon pain of death. Also, that no manner of persons, whatsoever they be, make no quarrel to any man, nor seize, nor vex, nor trouble any man, by body or goods, for any offence, or by colour of any offence heretofore done or committed against the Royal Majesty of the King our said Sovereign Lord, without his authority and especial commandment given unto him or them that so do in that behalf, upon pain of death. Also, that no manner of person nor persons whatsoever they be, ravish no religious woman, nor man's wife, daughter, maiden, nor no man's nor woman's servant, or take or presume to take any manner of victual, horsemeat, nor man's meat, without paying therefor the reasonable price thereof assessed by the clerk of the market, or other King's officers therefor ordained, upon pain of death."

Quarrelling, changing lodgings, interfering with civilians bringing food to the host were to be punished by imprisonment, and " his body to be at the King's will. And over this, that every man being of the retinue of our said Sovereign Lord, at the first sound or blast of the trumpet to saddle his horse ; at the second to bridle ; and at the third be ready on horseback to wait upon his highness, upon pain of imprisonment."

Eventually the forces met at Stoke, near Newark, and the King's artillery won. The battle lasted for some three hours. So heavy and uncertain was the fighting that reports were current in London that Henry had been defeated, and arrangements began privately to be made to greet and appease the conqueror. Even the Lieutenant of the Tower took steps. He had as one of his prisoners the Earl of Surrey, son of that Duke of Norfolk who was killed at Bosworth. He was a man of 43 at that time. The Lieutenant offered him his liberty ; the Earl refused to accept it. The King (he said—rather like St. Paul) had confined him and he would take his freedom only from the King. He even declared that, if Henry survived the defeat, he would offer him his allegiance. It is, of course, to be remembered that he certainly knew Simnel's claim to be Earl of Warwick was false, since the true Earl of Warwick was a co-prisoner in the Tower, and Warwick's fate if Simnel won must certainly be no less perilous than if Henry won. It was not for Surrey to abase the almost royal blood of the Howards, of whom he was now the head, to a known Pretender. Henry survived, to hear the story, to set Surrey free, and to use him. Surrey survived, to lead in a later year the King's forces in the north, to win Flodden in another reign, and to preside in that reign over the trial of the boy who was now Duke of Buckingham, thus again helping to establish the Tudors. As important perhaps as any of these deeds was the fact that he married his daughter Elizabeth to a rich retired city merchant Thomas Boleyn and thus became the grandfather of Anne Boleyn, whom his son and her uncle Thomas in turn helped to destroy.

Another incident in London, dependent on the false rumours of the King's defeat, was that the fugitives and criminals who had taken refuge in the liberties of Westminster gathered in a body and set out to plunder the houses of the gentlemen who were with the King. The riot was suppressed, but it gave rise to a letter of Henry's to the Pope which recounted a moral tale of the riot. The letter had two main points; one was to remind the Pope that the King had already written to him regarding the limitation if not the complete suppression of the privilege of sanctuary; the other was a request that the Pope should censure the Irish bishops who had supported the "spurious lad" Simnel, and issue to others "most positive precepts not to attack us thus flagitiously for the future." Between them was the story of one John Swit, a law-breaker as aforesaid, who made a mock of the anathema the Pope had threatened on any who had rebelled against Henry: "what signify censures of Church or Pontiff?" He had hardly spoken before "he instantly fell dead upon the ground, and his face and body immediately became blacker than soot itself, and shortly afterwards the corpse emitted such a stench that no one soever could approach it. Verily we give thanks to Almighty God who, of his ineffable mercy, has exhibited in our kingdom so great a miracle concerning the Christian faith." The King's piety accepted the story; his mind was of the sort that did. He passed his mind on to his son; the dead children of Katherine of Aragon seemed to Henry VIII as dreadful a portent of celestial displeasure as the black and stinking body of Swit could have seemed to Henry VII of celestial favour. The male Tudors were fretted by a superstitious anxiety, by the worse side of the Middle Ages, by a feverish waiting on God's signs. Their women were wiser. Mary escaped it in religion, Elizabeth in scepticism.

When the battle of Stoke ended, the rebels had been completely routed. Lincoln, the chosen heir of Richard, was killed with many other leaders. Lovell escaped, to die soon after in obscurity and perhaps starvation. Simnel and his master Symons were taken prisoner. Symons was sent to prison : Simnel was sent to the King's kitchens as a scullion, and afterwards promoted to be a falconer.

Such a judgment on the part of the King was neither quite mercy nor quite contempt. Henry was hardly the man to run any risks for the sake of either. He no more loved executions than he loved battles, but he never hesitated to execute. If he spared now, he spared because he judged rightly that Simnel was never likely to be a danger from the kitchens on his own initiative, and he thought he would himself gain more reputation from putting his enemies under his feet while they lived. It was a risk that was no risk if he had taken Simnel's measure rightly, and yet being no risk it did in some sense adorn the glory of the Prince that the Pretender should be so low. Henry by now was becoming a Prince of the Renascence ; the temper of the Renascence richly adored the Prince, and Henry had put himself in a position to be the Prince. He had exhibited himself as such; he had taken on a becoming magnificence; he was destroying his enemies. All these things, and others, combined to reassure men in England that authority still inhabited the Throne, and it was a habit of the time to delight in thinking that authority inhabited there as we in our time dislike and forbid the Throne to have authority. The Wars of the Roses had shaken the Throne, but now it was stable, and stable in the manner of the time. Lambert Simnel in the kitchen is a kind of symbol of the settled change in Henry's position. He was not only King, but (except for the vigil compelled by his own caution) he could for the moment take his ease in his Kingship.

It had, however, its inevitable political cares abroad as well as at home. The King returned to London to take them up. He had to deal with the other Princes, to decide upon friendship or hostility, or (more after his natural habit) to select neither and avoid both. But it was his first concern to be admitted, as it were, to the guild of Princes, and the manner of admission was, generally speaking, by marriage. The adored and adorned persons of the Kings sealed or initiated their achievements of policy by nuptials between their families, and to be allowed to marry or arrange a marriage into the pattern was to be recognized. Henry's own marriage had been a necessity of home politics though he had managed to make it seem a grace. He had no brothers or sisters of his own, and no connexions of his wife would strengthen his own position. It must be his and not her mortgage; to make use of her security would only exhibit his own poverty. Winchester supplied him with the means. The Prince Arthur was little more than a year old when his father began to make proposals for his future.

The chief members of the royal company of Europe with whom the Tudor had to deal were the rulers of Scotland, France, and Spain, and the King of the Romans. The King of Scotland at this time was James IV, a Stuart, and the direct descendant of that other James I who had been held a prisoner in the Tower by Henry IV. There he had seen Jane Beaufort, the daughter of the first Earl of Somerset, the illegitimate son of John of Gaunt, to whose house Henry VII himself belonged; his love for her was recorded in his own poem *The Kingis Quhair*. It is pleasant, among royal marriages of other kinds, to remember that beauty of love and verse:

> "And thus befell my blisfull aventure
> In youth of lufe, that now, from day to day,
> Flourith aye newe."

It is difficult to think of Henry VII engaging in a "blisful aventure" or indeed using the word "bliss," that strange substantive full of experience too intense to be called ethereal yet too alien to be endured. The poem which recorded it was dedicated to Gower and Chaucer; the death of its author was the theme of Rossetti's *King's Tragedy*. Of all the Scottish kings only James I's descendant, Mary Queen of Scots, has been so closely related to English poetry. It was his great-grandson who now sat on the Scottish Throne, a lad of fifteen, already engaged both in politics and war, whose own later love and death at Flodden move in the cantos of *Marmion*. He, like all the kings of Scotland, had to struggle with his barons; he was not so successful as Henry VII in overcoming them, but that was a little because Henry supported them. This was no particular vice on Henry's part; it was the habit of his age.

The King of France was almost as young as James IV; he was a boy of seventeen, and he was under the protection and tutelage of his very capable sister, Anne of Beaujeu. It was Anne who was maintaining the French Crown against inner treacheries and outer independences; it was Anne who was directing the threat against Brittany. There the old Duke was still alive, and still endeavouring to buy help with the hands of his daughters. One of the suitors now was that fascinating and disappointing figure, Maximilian, King of the Romans, who was the nearest of all to the supreme crown, more glorious if less certain than all the rest; the imperial diadem which still faintly recalled the effort of Charlemagne, the dream of Dante, the purpose of peace and justice, and the unity of Christendom. Less in effectiveness than before, it was in those years even larger in idea, for since the Eastern Empire had died with Palæologus at the fall of Constantinople, the Western Empire had become again the whole. But that supra-national and supernatural authority was becoming more of a dream than ever, and Maximilian was not the man to restore it.

He was the son of the Emperor Frederick III, and he was therefore the King of the Romans. In 1493 Frederick died. The Imperial dignity was elective and not hereditary, but it had become hereditary in effect. Maximilian was recognized as Emperor but never crowned; he was determined to be formally Emperor. Unfortunately he was also determined to be and to do everything else that his eyes fell on. He surged through Europe, militant, unreliable, impoverished, well-intentioned, self-destructive; "always in every feast and every fray, always wanting money and selling himself for promises, and never getting the money and never keeping his engagements; a good deal of the rake and a good deal of the knight-errant," wrote Bishop Stubbs. He was entangled in so many wars and alliances that his commitments were continually thwarting each other. He seems at last to have

THE KING AND THE KINGS 75

meant to make himself Pope instead of Emperor, and to have himself canonized before his death. Perhaps the most permanent thing he did was to ensure after him the succession of Charles V to the Empire. He would in no age have been of creative or constructive force, but he seems incongruous as well as futile in contrast with Ferdinand and Henry.

Henry's immediate problem, however, was not in the Central European sphere of influence, but in the French. In the days of his youth, in circumstances now, or so it was to be hoped, bygone, the exiled Tudor had owed shelter and help both to the Duke of Brittany and the King of France. It is true they had used him as a make-weight to Richard III, as (soon now) another Pretender was to be all-but-used against Henry. But Henry was willing to forget all that, now he was on the Throne. He held no grudge. It was always the immediate and future moments with which King Henry was concerned; the past he only used to be a convenience to the future. Nor could he have gained anything by maintaining a grudge. Ambassadors came to him from both. Some two months after Bosworth, in October 1485, he made a treaty with France for a year, and made the integrity and freedom of commerce a part of it. Three months afterwards it was renewed for three years. In July 1486 he concluded a similar treaty, with similar conditions, with Brittany. It was fairly clear, however, that these documents were but preliminaries. Free trading facilities with each of two angry opposites is not so easily gained.

War between the two Governments had already been in existence for some time. The Breton Government offered the hands of the old Duke's two daughters to the Imperial house; of Anne the elder to Maximilian, of Isabeau the younger to his son Philip, Archduke of Austria. Maximilian agreed to give assistance against the French. He was not able, however, to be of much direct use; Henry Tudor still remained a desirable ally. In 1488 the King at once avoided giving help to either power and yet made a demonstration of his own prestige and a sign of sympathy with both by offering to mediate. It was but three or four years since he had been a hanger-on at the ducal and royal courts. He now sent to both courts one of his servants, a man who had been concerned in the earliest proposals of the marriage with Elizabeth, a priest, Christopher Urswick. He has, more than most of these historic ghosts, a faint but substantial immortality, for he fleets once across the stage in Shakespeare's *Richard III* and speaks eight undistinguished lines. He fleeted now from England to Brittany and France; his proposal was accepted in the second and rejected in the first. The emigrant Duke of Orleans, who was fighting on the Breton side, sent him back not only with a high demand for help but with a reminder that the capture of the Breton coast-line by France would have undesirable results for England.

Urswick returned and was sent out again with renewed offers. The King, meanwhile, had determined to take certain steps at home. The feeling against the ancient enemy France was still high; half-following it and half-leading it, Henry made use of it. He collected a fleet and demanded supplies from his second Parliament " against the King's enemies." It was, however, the King's friends who were a greater immediate nuisance. The Queen's uncle, Edward, Lord Woodville, had been urging Henry to take action against France in defence of small nationalities. When the King seemed to be unobservant of his plea he determined to take action himself. He was Governor of the Isle of Wight; he collected several hundred men and moved them to Southampton. He embarked them there on a Breton ship and set sail. On the way across they met and seized a French ship, thus arriving in Brittany with the prestige of victory. England, it seemed, was gloriously coming in on the Breton side. Urswick, then in France on a message of mediation, found himself in personal danger. Unfortunately for the Bretons the victories did not continue. In July 1488 the French heavily defeated the Bretons; Woodville and most of his men were killed; the Duke of Orleans was taken prisoner; and the old Duke was compelled to make submission. He died immediately after, and his daughter Anne succeeded.

Another and a greater power than the "hot, hasty, and wild" Woodville was already in process of compelling Henry, against his will, to define himself as taking sides. His wish to avoid this was less than his wish to establish himself and his house among the Kings of Europe. The year 1488 saw the orientation of his policy—an orientation with a southward trend. He had, by then, two properties with which to bargain—England his realm, and Arthur his son. In a greater man those two names might have seemed titles of his being, aspects of his power. It is at once a lack and a capacity in Henry that they do not seem so in him. They appear as his belongings—or at least his belongings if he is fortunate—the matter of his contracts. He determined on the contract that would be best for himself and his company, and with care, industry, and skill he set to work to form an agreement. In March the embassy commissioned to breathe the word *marriage* left England for Spain.

It was not a new thing. Very little of Henry's policy, at home or abroad, was new; all that was new was its success. He took this proposal

THE KING AND THE KINGS 79

from the reign of Richard Plantagenet as he took a good many of his domestic measures from Edward Plantagenet. There had been a suggestion that Richard's son should marry a Spanish princess, and that the two countries should form a league against France. The new King wished to achieve the marriage while avoiding, if possible, the league against France. Unfortunately he had to deal with a very able man, assisted by a very able woman, with Ferdinand of Aragon and Isabella of Castile, sovereigns of Spain.

On 10th March the Prior of St. John of Jerusalem, the Dean of Wells, Christopher Urswick, and others received commission to conclude alliance with Ferdinand and Isabella. On 30th March the Spanish sovereigns sent their own ambassadors a commission to conclude a marriage between the Infanta Katherine and Arthur Prince of Wales. The Infanta had been born on 5th December 1485; the Prince of Wales on 20th September 1486. Each of them was two years old. When the King heard of the commission he " broke out " into a *Te Deum laudamus*. He appointed commissioners in England, who said the most important thing to discuss was not the alliance but the marriage, and the first thing was to settle the dowry. Pressed to name a sum they mentioned " —two hundred thousand gold scudos—every scudo to be of the value of 4s. 2d." They proposed that all the

Spaniards in London should be made security for the payment.

There was a discussion of some interest on this point. The Spaniards proposed to leave the whole matter to Ferdinand and Isabella, "who would behave with more liberality the more they were trusted." When the English demurred to this as "inconvenient," the first note of superiority is heard. "Bearing in mind what happens every day to the Kings of England, it is surprising," the ambassadors said, "that Ferdinand and Isabella should dare to give their daughter at all." This (they added) was said with great courtesy in order that they might not feel displeasure or be enraged. The English Commissioners abated one-third of their demand. Presently the English came down to a half; the Spaniards offered a fourth. The Spaniards, with the utmost courtesy, stressed the advantage the King of England would derive from the matter; later, in relation to the alliance, they again referred to sinister possibilities. "The greatness and prosperity of Spain," they said, "would contribute much to make that impossible which has happened so often, and which still happens, to the Kings of England. If the treaty of alliance were to be made public, tranquillity and order would be secured."

Against this argument the English produced reasons why the Spanish sovereigns should pay, which were three. (i) "The English asked why, as the money was not to come out of the strong-boxes of the King and Queen but out of the pockets of their subjects, they should not be more liberal." (ii) England, they said, "is a very dear place, and money is spent freely by the great people there." (iii) The great lords were "rich and prosperous"—they named a number—and there was not "a drop of blood in existence from which any danger might arise." They therefore refused to lessen their requests.

The discussion beneath the discussion was obvious; it was on the question: *How secure is the King of England?* It is clear from the whole account that the Spaniards did not consider the English as, politically, on the same level as themselves. They refer to Henry and the English as "doing the bidding" of Ferdinand and Isabella, and they regard the proposed marriage as ensuring peace and quiet in England. The English, refusing to consider it so, were yet at a disadvantage, for Simnel had been but lately defeated, and the Earl of Warwick was still in the Tower. Besides, considering how Henry had won the Throne, it was difficult to deny that such things *did* happen to the Kings of England. It was the reason that Henry was there to negotiate at all.

Leaving the matter of the marriage portion unsettled the commissioners passed on to the matter of the King of France. It was this with which the Spanish sovereigns were at bottom concerned. They wanted a clause inserted in the treaty binding Henry to go to war with France when he was told to, and not to make peace until certain provinces had been restored to both the Powers. The English objected both to the clause in itself and to its insertion in the treaty. The King would promise to do what the sovereigns needed, but he or his commissioners had moral objections to defining what that was. " The King of England has received many great services from the King of France, and it would not be honest to insert the clause against France. Such things are more justifiable and honest when done than when written."

The Spanish ambassador showed, so he reported to his master, that he was " scandalized and discontented " with this answer. A very odd ceremony followed. The Bishop of Exeter and his fellow-commissioners, in order to satisfy the Spaniards, swore on the missal before a crucifix " in the most solemn way " that it was the will of the King of England to do what he would by no means agree to formulating in the treaty that he would do. It was the written word to which he objected, whether lest it might somehow come to the knowledge of the King of France or whether it seemed to his own mind to commit him in a permanent record, whereas oaths (especially oaths by someone else) are only records in heaven, and can there, as most men feel, be explained or excused. Unlike heaven, the Spanish sovereigns were not satisfied with oaths. They were willing to omit the clause from the marriage treaty itself, but they insisted that then Henry must sign and swear to a secret treaty. A signed agreement they must have, and a move "at our bidding" by Henry against France.

The ambassadors were taken to see Arthur—first naked and then asleep. They discovered "such excellent qualities in the Prince as are quite incredible." Henry (almost like a proud father) wished drawings of him to be sent to Spain. Normally, however, he concealed his parental pride, as he concealed so much else, at least where he had it to conceal.

Efforts were made to establish a better understanding between Henry and Maximilian. The purpose of the Spanish sovereigns was to erect a great coalition against France; the purpose of Henry was to find out what Maximilian would give him if he abandoned most of his threat to Brittany. Eventually all the discussions worked themselves out as Ferdinand and Isabella intended that they should. Henry suffered a severe diplomatic defeat. It was a necessity, to his mind, that he should achieve the marriage for his son. If he must go to war with France to do it, well, he must go to war with France. He made the best of a bad job of which he had to make the best. He signed the dictated treaty of Medina del Campo. As soon as the existing truce with France expired, Henry was not to renew it unless Spain was a party. Neither party was to conclude a peace with France without the other unless the French gave up certain provinces—Normandy and Aquitaine to England, Roussillon and Cerdana to Spain. In that case either might make peace at once. Even in that clause, however, Henry's defeat was marked. Roussillon and Cerdana were outlying provinces, leased by Spain to France in 1462. Normandy and Aquitaine were important provinces which had belonged to England once and been retaken in war. It was quite certain that nothing but catastrophic defeat would cause the French to yield them, but much less than catastrophe might lead them to satisfy Ferdinand. The decision on peace was likely therefore to be Ferdinand's and not Henry's.

The diplomatic defeat being about to happen, the King set to work to nullify it. "His Majesty," wrote the Papal Collector in January 1489, "added that he was compelled to defend the Breton interests, both on account of the immense benefits conferred on him by the late Duke in the time of his misfortunes and likewise for the defence of his own kingdom . . . He was determined to defend Brittany and the orphan Duchess with all his might." His embassy was at that moment in Brittany. He compelled the orphan to surrender to him as security for his expenses two towns, to carry over his army at her expense and in her ships, to promise to aid Henry in recovering Normandy, etc., and even the French Throne if desired, and not to marry without Henry's consent. The orphan sighed and signed; she was even more in need of the King of England's soldiers than he of the King of Spain's daughter. In order to assist the orphan he took advantage of anti-French feeling at home to make his vantage upon his Parliament, to extract a heavy grant "against the ancient enemies."

The presumed patriots at home were no more grateful than the harassed Duchess abroad. There was a rising of the people in the North against the subsidy which was to be spent by the King, had been voted by Parliament, and must be supplied in the end by them. The Earl of Surrey was sent against them; the King followed; the rebels fled. The King took the usual royal vengeance, and continued to profess the highest moral beauty of purpose. Between 1489 and 1492 the general negotiations which had been proceeding between the King of England, the King and Queen of Spain, and the King of the Romans, were assisted by military movements.

Forces were sent over to Brittany, certain small victories won, and certain small towns taken or surrendered. The war gave tone to the negotiations; it could hardly do more. The Pope sent envoys to beg the Christian kings to combine against the encroaching Turk. The sovereigns of Spain drove the Moors out of the country by at last taking Granada. The Duchess had sufficient experience of the benefactors of the orphan. In 1491, desperate and hopeful, she turned to her enemy. She determined, if she must lose Brittany, to lose it in a high manner; she would not surrender it but unite it. She accepted the French King's offer, threw over Maximilian her betrothed husband, and married Charles of France himself.

Henry, for once in his careful life, seems to have been thoroughly annoyed. " Such intense and insatiable coveting of the dominions of others," he wrote to the Pope, " cannot be borne . . . it might inflict some trouble and injury on your Holiness and the Apostolic See." He had been making military preparations and he had been raising subsidies for the war. He could not drop the whole idea merely because the French had achieved their purpose ; now rather was the time when he must use his preparations. He passed over to France in October 1492, with an army of some twenty-seven thousand men, and landed at Calais, from which he moved towards Boulogne. At Boulogne he was offered a large payment by the French King if he would go home—seven hundred and twenty-five thousand gold crowns in fifteen yearly instalments. It was not Normandy and Aquitaine, but Henry had never wanted Normandy and Aquitaine; he found the crowns much more credible and much more intelligent. He had gained more than he had supposed he could; out of the nettle of Medina del Campo he had plucked the flower of hard cash. He signed the treaty on 3rd November; it seems not to have been popular. The army returned to England.

The King wrote to the Pope Alexander VI (newly elected that year) that "a peace was proposed to us by the French with such conditions as to make it appear that no Christian and Catholic prince could be capable of refusing them"—any of the seven hundred and twenty-five thousand of them. He added: "We accepted this peace, both in order to attend to other matters and to avoid shedding Christian blood." He was probably wholly accurate.

CHAPTER IV

THE MULTIPLICATION OF THE KING

HENRY Tudor had fled to Brittany when he was fourteen. He had landed there in 1471, and lived there during the last twelve years of Louis XI of France, who had died in 1483. In 1484 Henry had fled to France and remained there for another year, till August 1485. Part of that time he had spent under restraint; all of it in a consideration of his own chances. But he had also an opportunity to contemplate, from a distance, the operation of the French crown in its own land.

He had before him an object-lesson, the same lesson that his own life, by the time of his coronation, had taught him. He had heard of Louis XI's victories over the great lords, and both seen and heard of Anne of Beaujeu's struggles with them on behalf of her brother, the minor Charles. He had seen and heard of the power of the Duke of Orleans, and how it hampered the Regency. His own accession to the Throne, so far and unlikely as it had at first seemed, had taken place because the Kings of England had not managed to control the lords; to whom he had himself been, except

MULTIPLICATION OF THE KING 89

in the one great strait, rather one of themselves than a scion of royalty.

At the very States-General which were in session when he reached France, he became aware of a thing he had not formally known before. In Wales during the wars he had not had much opportunity of discovering the general state of the people, and Brittany was concerned with other things. But the States-General were compelled to listen to violent protests about the general state of the people, and especially about the evils done by the soldiery. The state of things in England, even during the wars of the Roses, was doubtfully as bad. In France there had been no opportunity to lighten the oppression of the lower classes. The royal revenue was always below its needs. The extortion of money was one of the chief royal habits, and the extortion of money was a chief cause of desolation. Taxes and brigandage—legal and illegal tyranny—might ruin too much the basis of the Throne. It had been clear to him that a successful ruler in England would have a difficult problem.

There is little to show that Henry was sympathetic in mind towards the poor as such, and nothing at all to show that he was unselfish. But, like Charles II, he had no mind to go again on his travels. The surest way of making certain that he would not do so was to multiply himself by his agents; so that by seeming to be contemporaneously himself (by means of others) in every place he avoided the long sequence of being only himself in renewed exile. He desired a contented country; as far as possible his work-people must be satisfied. He was always prepared to crush strikes and riots, but he was mildly prepared to give bonuses to hard workers, especially if they were *his* hard workers and had little to do with the other directors on the Board.

He had France in front of his eyes. In fact, however, he had no need to call on France for examples which the past history of his own land provided. Edward IV, who had made a similar attempt, had frankly been defeated by the lords. There had been reasons for it. Henry proceeded to show those reasons where they got off and he got on. A beneficent despotism—which is what he aimed at—has two chief difficulties: its agents and its successor. Henry was fortunate, at first, in the first; less fortunate in the second. But then it was too late for him to worry.

The Lancastrian dynasty had been compelled to keep on good terms with the lords—with the Families of that day. The Plantagenet revival under Edward and Richard had attempted to break that tradition, already encouraged by the falling value of money and the needs of the Crown. Henry did not so much attempt to break as to nullify. He rather made it his business to see that Parliament wanted what he wanted than to impose what he wanted on Parliament. To us, nowadays, no doubt the distinction between King and Parliament seems only a shade of difference between two possessing powers. But even so, one was likely to be better than the other, and Henry had determined which should be.

"It is not for nothing," says Miss Temperley in her careful study of the King, "that the word 'Majesty' first appears in this reign." The King multiplied his majesty. The most significant step was taken in 1487. Henry established, in a quite particular sense, the King's Justice; *i.e.* he created his own special Court of Law. It was not, it seemed, sufficient to compel Parliament to take oaths to control itself. Parliament was as likely to fail there as most individuals do. The ordinary courts of justice were weak and likely to be overawed by the great peers. Robbery and murder remained on the increase. Liveries and maintenance still marched about the country. Sheriffs and juries were threatened and bribed. Sanctuary was a refuge, benefit of clergy an escape. Often, no doubt, the refuge was justified and the escape just; the innocent in those days—as in all—cannot have stood much of a chance once they had been seized by authority, except by great good luck. But from the point of view of the central civil government they were both merely a nuisance, and the fact that neither the King's group of clergy nor the advisers to the

Holy See thought it desirable to fight for them, suggests that the abuse was recognized to be disproportionate.

Innocent VIII assented to the King's petition so far as to allow the royal guards to surround and keep the sanctuary in cases of persons accused of treason. It is tempting to see in this Bull an example of the rise of the person of the Prince, which had now become so sacred that the sanctuary could hardly save the man who threatened it. Unfortunately in 1504 the Bull was supplemented by another which made the same provision for all criminals, and forbade any offender who had once taken sanctuary, and escaped and repeated the offence, to be allowed the advantage of such rescue a second time. We cannot therefore allow ourselves the pretence. Yet something like that was in fact happening, and the difference between medieval monarchy and Renascence monarchy involves a change of style. It is not alone in England that the Prince becomes a kind of god upon earth, whereas he had before been (like the Pope) the vassal of God upon earth. It seems to burst on us in England in the person of Henry VIII, because Henry VIII, partly by his temperament, partly by his loves, partly by the religious controversy, was spectacular. Henry VII was not, and one of our difficulties with him is to unite the least spectacular of men with the most spectacular of functions.

MULTIPLICATION OF THE KING 93

Sanctuary then was limited. But the effectual sanctuaries of the households of the great lords were as dangerous to ordered national government as the sanctuaries of the Abbeys. The Pope subdued the second at Henry's request. He himself subdued the first. He proceeded, now and through his reign, to take measures which controlled and goaded local government. He took great care to compel localities to consume, as it were, their own murderers, too many of whom habitually escaped, " to the great displeasure of the King." He caused bail to be tightened. Coroners who neglected inquests were fined; townships who were responsible for the escape of criminals were fined. A slow and difficult hunting down of murder went on all over the country all through the reign.

The chief operation, however, was that recreation of the King's own court. There had been in the days of Henry VI a power given to the King's Privy Council to summon rioters before it. It sat in the room of Westminster called the Star Chamber to exercise this special jurisdiction. This had, not unnaturally, ceased to work during the Rose wars. It was now revived, with a difference. In old days the Star Chamber sat to exercise extraordinary powers bestowed upon it *ad hoc* by the King. Henry determined that the King in his Star Chamber should be an ordinary rather than an extraordinary thing—a normal instead of an abnormal. The King was not only to be the origin of law in his person; he was to be the exercise of law by his creation. Judges were to be involved in it, but it was to depend primarily not on judges but on the King's ministers. The Chancellor, the Treasurer, and the Privy Seal, or any two of them, summoning to their company and acting in concert with a bishop and a lay peer from the Council, were also to summon two judges (preferably the Chief Justices of the King's Bench and of Common Pleas). The stress of such a court would obviously be on the King's side, since its nucleus and its initiative lay in the King's officers, and at least two (and possibly more) of the other members were to be chosen by the King's officers. It was to act as if in ordinary process of law; it could receive information, summon, examine, convict, punish. The direct intention was for the " policy and good rule of the realm." It was meant chiefly to control men in high place and men in positions of royal trust. It was to control and abolish " unlawful maintenance, giving of liveries, signs, tokens, and retainders, by indenture, promises, oaths, writing or otherwise." It was to watch " the untrue demeanings of Sheriffs," " taking of money by juries," " great riots and unlawful assemblies." It was to prevent the failure of " the laws of the land in execution " and the increase of the " unsureties of all men living."

Henry knew as much about unsurety as most of his subjects. He thought it desirable to remove this, even if it were only that their surety might support his own. In the next century but one it was determined that the King's security was not a necessary part of the government of England, any more than the security of his people was a necessary part of its aim. It was then determined that the laws of England should be at the commandment of Shallow and Simple and their betters, but not at Falstaff's or the King's—that the King should be dismissed on sufficient evidence of misbehaviour. The lawyers went with the Families and not with the King, and English law became far more of a closed doctrine than perhaps it would otherwise have done. For it developed without that consciousness of a side glance at itself, without the mirror in which it might have to contemplate itself — the Star Chamber of the King's personal choice. No doubt it gained much by doing so, but it lost something. Very likely things would have been no better if they had been different. But they are not different, and they are no better than they might have been. The odd thing is that we have reached to-day a state in which the King's ministers without the King do exactly what the King was, in the seventeenth century, blamed for doing: they control, create, and almost disregard law. It is true that, to some extent, the general habit of the English tends to modify the arbitrary orders made by Government. "In England," wrote Lenin, "there is powerful popular control over the administration, but even there that control is far from being complete, even there the bureaucracy has managed to preserve not a few of its privileges, is not infrequently the master, and not the servant, of the people."[1] He was wrong only on one point; he supposed it to be a bourgeois creation, but it is the bourgeoisie largely who have to put up with it.

Thus then in 1487 the King multiplied himself. The history of his reign is of a change in the kind of multiplication — from Morton and Fox to Empson and Dudley. But the multiplication was strictly his own; *plus ça change, plus c'est la même chose.* It was the King everywhere, and King Henry at that. He established the ostentatious habit of his dynasty, and, what is more, he carried it out. His servants were content to be faithful. His policy was not deflected or defeated by them under pretext of obedience. Both the next generations suffered because their servants were different, and the policy of Henry VIII and of Elizabeth was at times changed by that conscientious or unconscientious infidelity.

The establishment of the Star Chamber in 1487 and the recovery from Medina del Campo in 1491

---

[1] *The Tasks of Russian Social-Democrats.* Selected Works. Vol. i. Lawrence and Wishart. 1936.

are the marks of the increasing power and prestige of the Tudor. They preceded his most serious danger—the coming of Perkin Warbeck. But first there is another kind of multiplication to be, at least, remarked; it is that which can be called indifferently the Secret Service or the Spy System of the King.

There was, of course, nothing new about this, and in Renascence Europe nothing unusual. Henry himself suffered from it, or rather from the same principle in other hands. His lords and councillors were always apt to be receiving pay from foreign sovereigns. What is remarkable about Henry is that he seems to have saved himself from being dependent on his spies. They were not encouraged to think they had been particularly useful. Money payments are recorded to them; he was no more miserly on them than on his jewels, though indeed both spies and jewels served the same purpose, they were both a part of the King's behaviour. It is unlikely he ever passed a false jewel; unlikely that he ever paid an unreliable spy. He watched and checked the reports. It was felt that it was unsafe to bring tales to him without proof; he was said to be "hard of credence." He interrogated his spies and slanderers with a cunning greater than their own; he was apt, they said, to suppose such things to be said " of envy, ill-will, and malice." So, no doubt, they were, but as one reads it is difficult to avoid the belief that the King's incredulity was as much diplomatic as noble, that his reluctance to accept stories of intrigue and his difficult interrogatories were as much to extract the whole tale as to free the accused person from suspicion. He was ruled rather by a cautious determination to know the facts than by any passionate fear. He remained the master of his spies, and kept them also in dependence. But it was they who enabled the King to spread his power abroad. In 1499 the Milanese ambassador wrote to his Duke, on the arrest of an English rebel in France : " This thing will be held of great account by his Majesty . . . as the English may say : ' Whither shall I go then from thy spirit or whither shall I flee from thy presence ? ' "

Had he no friends ? Bacon's sentences seem to deny it : " He was governed by none. His Queen . . . could do nothing with him. His mother, whom he reverenced much, heard little. For any person agreeable to him for society . . . he had none." Yet there seems, oddly enough, to be a possibility that he may have had something like *one*, though he is difficult to discern. In the Introduction to the *Calendar of Spanish State Papers* (published in 1862), by G. A. Bergenroth, is a study of the Spanish Ambassador to Henry, Rodrigo Gonsalvi de Puebla. Of this man Bergenroth says : " Henry, in gaining over the affections of De Puebla, became attached to

MULTIPLICATION OF THE KING 99

him in a degree uncommonly high for his character. There were sufficient indications that Henry trusted to De Puebla more than he would confide to any other ambassador. It is even probable that at that time there was not a single Englishman who shared the confidence of the King to so great an extent. . . . Both Henry and De Puebla had few, if any, real friends, but they were attached to each other to a degree rarely seen among better men."

It is a suggestion of very great interest. De Puebla was in England during most of the reign. He came here first in about 1487; he was recalled in 1489. In 1494 he was sent over again; he was here when the King died, and he himself died here soon after. He was made the Master of Sherborne Hospital, and his son became a Canon of St. Paul's. He was retained here by Ferdinand and Isabella in spite of the reports concerning him transmitted to the sovereigns by other envoys and merchants. If these accounts are to be even half believed, De Puebla was a man of low character, greedy in every sense of the word, mean, dishonest, deceitful, and even treacherous. He was originally a doctor of civil and canon law from Andalusia, and he came to England in connexion with the first negotiations concerning the marriage. Henry is reported to have realized that the Spanish sovereigns did not know the kind of man they were sending. "De Puebla," wrote another Spanish envoy, " wished to ingratiate himself with Henry." He therefore naturally began to magnify to his rulers the difficulties in the way of the marriage ; the prestige of Henry at the Court of Spain depended largely on the assurances of De Puebla. It is scarcely surprising that Henry began to entertain a careful affection for any attention to the Ambassador. " King Henry is certainly satisfied with De Puebla not because he thinks him a good man or a good servant of the King and Queen of Spain, but because he carries on negotiations rather in the interests of England than Spain." This was an opinion written in 1498 by other Spaniards ; in 1507 the Princess Katherine wrote to her father : " De Puebla is more a vassal of the King of England than a servant of your Highness." It is unlikely that De Puebla thought so. He himself wrote that he was the most trustworthy servant the King of Spain had ; he had spent his property in the King's service and begged, at least, that his salary might be paid. It is very likely that, if the other opinion were in effect true, there would be set up between Henry and De Puebla a relationship more subtle than either knew. Henry perhaps despised De Puebla. But he did not despise Spain. De Puebla perhaps fawned on Henry. But the Spain behind him did not fawn. " The King of England," wrote De Puebla in 1507, " has no confidential adviser." It seems likely that in

Spanish affairs he had one—De Puebla—" he really became the English minister for foreign affairs as far as Spain and Flanders were concerned " (*Cal. Span. State Papers*, Introd.).

King Henry gave De Puebla very little except liking, if that. It was not altogether, for once, his fault. He offered him a bishopric ; he offered him a rich wife. In each case the offer had to be referred to Spain, and in each case the sovereigns remained awfully silent. De Puebla pestered them a little, but he was defeated. In each case he thanked them for having taken no notice. They continued to take no notice.

It is an odd picture ; that of the half-contemptuous King of England allowing himself to grow slowly intimate with the Spanish ambassador, and such an ambassador ! He lived, it is said, in an inn of small reputation ; he sat at the common table and was friendly with apprentices. His landlord cheated his clients, and the name of the Spanish ambassador protected him. The English Court, even the King, laughed at him. He was always trying to dine at the Palace. The Queen allowed herself once to ask if his Castilian master did not provide him with food. On another occasion the King himself asked why De Puebla was coming to see him ; a rash voice answered : " To eat." The King laughed.

But he was retained in his place. Other Spanish ambassadors came and went—except the

Princess Katherine who only came. She, who hated him, denounced him to her father continually. But Ferdinand would neither remove De Puebla nor content De Puebla. Only in the last letter addressed to his ambassador he said he was sorry he had been ill and had given orders that his financial affairs should be attended to. No one ever worked for less personal profit—unwillingly ; it would be a fitting Henrician friendship.

CHAPTER V

"HE OF YORK"

AT the moment when Henry Tudor had arranged a marriage with Spain and a peace with France, the vision of a revolting England rose out of the Western seas. At the moment when he might be said to have established himself as indeed King, the living myth of a more legitimate King circulated through the courts of Europe. Even now there lingers in the histories not merely an account of the episode, but an argument, and the claims of the greatest of the Pretenders are disproved to-day as earnestly (or as reluctantly) as they were in the England of the fifteenth century. Certainly Henry had a little bad luck in that matter, for a century or so after his death it pleased John Ford to write a tragedy on Perkin Warbeck—a tragedy with something of the passion of love, heroism, and death in its concluding scenes. Such things are not without their effect on the general imagination of history. "The willing suspension of disbelief" exercised at one point is a fact of our experience, and must have its results on our experience. It is this "willing suspension" which the censorship (of whatever body) refuses to allow us, and it is difficult to deny that it may be right—if that suspension may produce harmful results, and if it is certain that our censors know what is harmful and what is not. Ford made Warbeck noble in art; no one ever put Henry VII into art at all.

There are of course historical reasons for the importance of Warbeck; the chief of them is Margaret, Dowager Duchess of Burgundy. The next is a result of the whole affair—the execution of the unfortunate Earl of Warwick. It was a crisis, and a crisis after which Henry seems to have been changed. In that pattern of faint lines which are all we can—with such doubts—discern of his mind and soul, there seems to be a deepening and thickening here and there. When the news of Warbeck first reached the King he was thirty-six; when Warbeck was executed, he was forty-three. The seven years episode fretted the lines of his character more deeply. He surrendered himself to some element in his heart. He became himself. " In him, as in all men (and most of all in kings) his fortune wrought upon his nature, and his nature upon his fortune," wrote Bacon: the chief junction of them was at this crisis, and their union in its resolution.

Perkin Warbeck's origin is known chiefly by the confessions that he read in public after he had been taken prisoner by Henry VII. They have always therefore seemed a little suspect, since they were certainly the kind of confessions that were most useful to the King. But they may be true, for all that, since they were uncontradicted by any evidence other than Warbeck's own statements at an earlier period, and since the very few exterior phrases which are of any use at all seem to confirm them. According to them, Perkin was born about 1474 or 1475, in Tournai. His father was a controller of customs, and he and the mother were well-known persons—John Warbeck (or Osbeck) and Katherine de Faro. He lived in Flanders, serving various masters, until 1489, when he came into the household of a certain Lady Frampton, the wife of Sir Edward Frampton. Sir Edward had been a strong Yorkist, and not only that but he had gained his knighthood, with lands and promises of other favours, for his good services at the time of the Duke of Buckingham's rebellion. The overthrow of Richard III sent the Framptons into flight. Lady Frampton was leaving for Portugal, and she took Warbeck with her. He had a curiosity, he said, to see the world, and in Lisbon, having spent a year with another master, a one-eyed knight called Peter Varz de Cogna, he joined a Breton merchant then sailing for Ireland. There the two of them arrived in 1490 or 1491. It was in 1491 that another Henry Tudor was born in England.

In Ireland his appearance caused something like a sensation. The confessions rather imply that the Yorkist leaders were merely waiting for a convenient false claimant. But such a one would have been easy enough to find ; there must have been something distinctive about Warbeck which made him particularly suitable. He was remarkably good looking ; he had admirable bearing and manners ; he had—he must have had—some kind of resemblance to Edward IV. He appeared, that is, like a young gentleman who could easily be believed to be the son of the debonair and handsome King of England. People who had every opportunity for judging right, accepted him. We cannot tell, at that time, how far he accepted himself. It is probable that he did. He was now sixteen or seventeen, and it is an age when one may be anything. On the other hand he seems to have refused to be anything but the possible greatest. He swore he was not the son of Richard III or the Duke of Clarence. He would not be persuaded to be Warwick; he consented to imagine himself to be Richard, Duke of York, the second son of Edward IV. His friends " made me to learn English and taught me what I should do and say."

The Anglo-Irish lords accepted him. The Earl of Desmond supported him ; the Earl of Kildare later was accused that he also " should have lain with the French lad . . . and that I should aid, support, and comfort him," which he denied. But, Kildare or no Kildare, the support given him was sufficient to make him a Pretender of standing. He was as dangerous as ever Henry Tudor had been at the same age, and (if he had any right) he had undoubtedly a better right to the Throne than Henry; he was the King in a sense in which Henry had never been. Whether indeed he was, depended and depends on unknown things. But there is about all the episodes a faint air of strange opposition. He is not the King, yet he is more the King than Henry, as if the King that Henry might have wished to be and could not, the spirit and image of the gay, handsome young King of ancestral right, as if the Plantagenet had escaped into this other incarnation. Even Henry's own acts rose to rebuke him; he saw that when he had dated his reign from the day before Bosworth he had encouraged any now doubtful adherents of his own to plunge into the immediate danger and possible future security of rallying to his enemy. He was not alone, for he had his servants; but he had not given himself to any of them, and therefore he was alone.

From Ireland the new Pretender sent out letters. He wrote, assisted by the Earl of Desmond, to the King of Scotland. But a grander gate was opened to him. In 1492, while Henry was preparing, rather against his will, to defend the cause of the fatherless Duchess, the equally fatherless King of France invited Warbeck to France. He had heard of his claim, and he wished to collect his claim and use it against

Henry, as Henry had been used to threaten Richard. The Pretender arrived; he was given a royal welcome (in the literal sense). He was treated, with all but open acknowledgements, as the rightful monarch, until the *de facto* King of England allowed himself to be bought off with crowns. The usual clause about neither side harbouring rebels and supporting them was contained in that Treaty. Without ceasing to believe in the Pretender's claims, the King of France invited the Pretender to leave French territory. There was one obvious refuge—the court of the Dowager Duchess of Burgundy—and there Warbeck went. It was a gamble. If the Duchess rejected him, all was over; if she accepted him, he would be confirmed in his claims. He passed north.

She *might* have refused. She did not. Her implacability or her credulity professed to discern in this young man the features of her brother Edward Plantagenet. She took him as her nephew. He was "the Prince of England, the White Rose." Though by far the most important she was not only the only convert. Maximilian, King of the Romans, allowed his knight-errantry and his dislike of Henry to persuade him also. The Pretender, then and long after, was "the Duke of York" to Maximilian; his son, the Archduke Philip, concurred in his father's decision. Already, therefore, the claimant was being received almost spontaneously into the guild of Princes.

The Spanish sovereigns were slower. In 1493 the White Rose wrote from Flanders to Isabella of Castile. He declared that his elder brother the Prince of Wales had been assassinated, and that he himself had been delivered " to a gentleman who had received orders to destroy him, but who, taking pity on his innocence, had preserved his life, and made him swear on the sacraments not to disclose for a certain number of years his birth and lineage." He had led a wandering, secret, and miserable life for eight years under the tutelage of two custodians. One of these died; the other returned to England. He himself was then in Portugal; he went to Ireland, and was there acknowledged. He was also acknowledged by the Kings of France, Denmark, Scotland, and of the Romans, by the Archduke, and many others. From England many had sent to him, all who were shocked by the iniquity of the usurper Henry of Richmond. Let the Queen Isabella intercede with her husband to give him the assistance which is his desire. He signed "Richard Plantagenet, second son of the late King Edward and Duke of York." In the Spanish chancery the letter was twice endorsed: " From Richard Plantagenet, called King of England," and " From Richard who styles himself King of England."

The letter is dated 8th September 1493. The Spanish sovereigns took no notice. In November of the same year the Pretender, finding himself at no greater advantage than when he first came to the Duchess, left her and went into Austria, to the court of Maximilian. In Vienna, as in Paris, he was royally received, and in the next year Maximilian permitted or encouraged a small magnificence of show. The arms of the Prince of Wales were displayed at his house; a guard of archers was assigned to him, and liveries of the White Rose. It was a gesture of anger and contempt towards Henry, but the realism with which the young man's claims were received everywhere is a sufficient suggestion of the carelessness of the European Kings about Henry. The picturesque heir of Plantagenet was more than a match for the rather dull diplomatic figure of the Tudor.

Meanwhile the Tudor was in process of action, moving in check to his various potential adversaries. If other powers without England or within used Warbeck as a threat he too would use him; to support Warbeck should be to feel the hostility of the King of England. He would even sacrifice the very thing he was anxious to encourage most —trade; the interests of the national company to the interests of the Chairman. He had written to Maximilian complaining of the attitude of the Dowager Duchess. Maximilian replied civilly, but declaring that the Duchess, within limits, was a free sovereign. He could not interfere. Henry determined to interfere as much as he could. Flanders was within his commercial reach. In September 1493 he forbade all intercourse between the two countries, and he expelled all Flemings from England. It was one of his rasher acts; it did no good politically and it did a good deal of harm economically. There was a riot in London, owing to the fact that the Hanse merchants could still trade with Flanders when the English were forbidden. " The Tuesday before St. Edward's Day in the morning, at 6 of the clock, was certain servants of the Mercers assembled, and went down to the Steelyard [1] and there would have despoiled the place; and, or the Mayor came and the Sheriffs, there gathered unto them a great people, some to take their part and some to behold; but the merchants had warning thereof and kept the gates shut; and as soon as the Mayor came, anon they fled as well from the water as from the gate. And divers were taken and sent to prison. And after search made it was found that two of John Picton's servants were beginners of this matter, which were taken; and after their examination they accused other persons, among the which number was not one householder, but

[1] " The Steelyard was the house of the merchants of the Thames, by Cairn Lane in Thames Street, on the site of the present Cannon Street Station." *Chronicles of London.* C. L. Kingsford. Clarendon Press. 1905.

all servants, and their more part apprentices and children."

Henry insisted on a strict inquiry by the City into the riot. But the unrest continued. In the following February four men were arrested for setting up placards in the City against the King's person and the Council. One claimed sanctuary and was remanded; three were executed at Tyburn. It was not however till the end of the year that the King was able to strike at higher game. By then he had information from his secret service and he had bought traitors. There was a certain Sir Robert Clifford who had been with the army in France, and had been an interpreter during the peace negotiations. Later he had come into contact with Warbeck, and had declared that he recognized the face of the Pretender, and had no doubt at all that he was Richard, Edward's son. He was in Flanders with the Pretender. On 22nd December 1494 there was issued in England a pardon for Sir Robert Clifford and a pardon for his servant Richard Waltier, of Aspenden, in Hertfordshire, gentleman. In January 1494-5 a grant of £500 was made to the same Robert Clifford. By then the first important blow had been aimed. In November the King had formally created the young Henry Duke of York; the Pretender was not to be allowed even that claim. Great triumphs and jousts were held at Westminster, " honourable and comfortable to the King and Queen and many other great estates there present to behold, and great gladness to all the common people." This celebration of the royal stability was followed by an exhibition of the royal power. Three leading clerics—the Dean of St. Paul's, the Provincial of the Black Friars, and the Prior of Langley—were arrested on charges of high treason, along with a number of lay persons of standing. The clerics were imprisoned, and pardoned the next year; the laics were executed. Clifford's evidence, however, was meant for the destruction of a greater than these. One of the heroes of Bosworth, Sir William Stanley, had been made an official intimate of the man he had helped put on the Throne; he was Chamberlain to the King. His brother was the husband of the King's mother, though that relationship cannot have meant much to him or to the King. Either from conviction, from caution, or from some unknown discontent, William Stanley followed that prevailing habit of the gentry; he had been attracted to correspondence with Warbeck. The correspondence had gone through Robert Clifford. Henry came to know of it, and for two years or so he permitted the treason to proceed. " He gathered upon him more and more." It is perhaps the length of time that makes the vigil seem dreadful; the vigil that ends at last with the seduction of Stanley's confidant, his purchase and pardon, and then with the arrest. It is the length of time, the careful operation, and the lack of any but a personal cause for the operation. In other years as much time and effort were spent, under Elizabeth, say, in catching traitors. But that work is coloured to us by the appearance of religion and the safety of the State. No goodwill of imagination has yet succeeded in identifying Henry VII with the salvation of the state; he concealed himself too much. How can England be identified with the King without a face? The face of Warbeck was, on Sir Robert Clifford's earlier showing, the face of Richard, Duke of York, and son of King Edward. Even if Warbeck and Clifford lied there is at least the brilliant lie to stare at; in England there are only the King's hands counting out five hundred pieces of gold.

It is his misfortune; in effect the peace and prestige of England did depend very largely on Henry, and in Henry's mind they depended on the gold. We English have, as it were, to be content to be saved by such unpleasing methods. Stanley was arraigned in Westminster Hall "before the lords," condemned, and sentenced. On Monday, 16th February 1494-5, "about six of the clock" he was beheaded on Tower Hill. " This was a man of great weight in his country," wrote the chronicler, " and a great man of moveable goods. In so much as the common fame ran that in his castle of Holt was found in read coin and plate and jewels to the value of forty thousand marks or more; and his land and fee extended to three thousand pounds by year." The King took all; his five hundred pounds had brought him a good increase. But he paid for the funeral. He even did something for Stanley's servants. He was neither cruel nor vengeful; it makes him, oddly, the more terrifying. The Earl of Derby, once Lord Stanley, brother of William, and the other hero of Bosworth, continued in all his offices; he had played his treason once and was content.

Certainly some consideration must be given to the things that were told the King by his spies. A year after he read a document, and endorsed it in his own hand: "La Confession de Bernart de Vignolles." It is an example of the kind of thing it was thought worth while reporting. No action seems to have been taken on it; perhaps it may be assumed that Henry did not believe it. But that it reached him at all seems to show that he was thought capable of believing it. In the midst of the serious diplomatic documents, the modern negotiations, the age-long habits of government, all those things we can so easily understand, comes, as natural as they, this document from another world. It begins:

"The deposition made by Bernard de Vignolles of the affair of Sir John Kendal, Grand Prior of the Order of St. John of Rhodes, Sir John Thonge, his nephew, a knight of the said Order, Master Archdeacon Hussey (of London), John Hussey his nephew, one named Lilly, and one named Waters, two servants of the said Archdeacon, and one named William Outon, secretary to the said Prior of St. John, all knowing of the enterprise undertaken by the said Prior of St. John, and Sir John Thonge, and the Archdeacon Hussey, all three being in Rome."

These three clerics, according to Vignolles, were seeking some way to kill the King of England, his children, his mother, and those who were near his person or of his Council. They got into touch with a Spanish astrologer Rodrigo, who persuaded the Archdeacon to take lodgings in his house for the better planning of what was obviously no small enterprise. But Rodrigo proved unsuccessful in plotting satisfactorily; the conspirators searched Rome for a better instrument and found yet another astrologer, also of Spain, a Master John, " which Master John, hearing their request, answered that he very well knew how to do what they wanted." They were in the splendid and cultured Rome of the Borgias. Master John demanded a sum of money from his clients, but he gave them evidence of his power : " for a greater proof that he could do what they wanted, he caused the death of a Turk, who was the servant of the brother of the Grand Turk, then held at Rome in the Pope's palace." Alexander VI was holding in his palace the Prince Zem, brother of the Emperor

Bajazet, half as a hostage, half as a threat. " And if the said three personages would deliver the money, the said astrologer promised he would do as they wished."

The said three personages, still according to Vignolles, were compelled to return to England—partly to raise the necessary funds—before the astrologer had begun his labours ; but they left a servant of the Grand Prior, a Sardinian named Stephen, to watch their interests. A deposit on account of the money was delivered *par banque*, but two years went by and the conspirators had not heard from their astrological murderer. What they did hear, to their unpleasant surprise, was that the first astrologer had been babbling. He was going about Rome saying that the Prior of St. John and the Archdeacon of London were planning to kill the King. The Prior and the Archdeacon, in common accord, determined to suppress the first astrologer and quicken the second. They sent Bertrand de Vignolles out to Rome on the double errand. He was to warn Master John that he would get no more cash till he had done something.

The astrologer offered to come to England, but this was thought inconvenient. So before Bernard returned he was given a little wooden box in which was an ointment. Bernard was to tell the Grand Prior to spread the ointment over any door or passage where the King might go. If this were done, those who most loved the King would be those who would kill the King. Bernard, having got back to his own lodgings, opened the box, and saw (as was only to be expected, according to the best rules of such romantic conspiracies) that the ointment was loathsome and stinking stuff. He threw it away—into a suitable place. The next day he set out on his return. When he had got as far as Orleans (it is still his own account) he was struck by the idea that the astrologer might have written to the Grand Prior saying what he had done, in which case the said Bernard might find himself in difficulties. He went therefore to an apothecary's and bought another little wooden box and some quicksilver. He concocted, with the quicksilver, a little dry earth, the sweat of his shirt, and water, something like the original article, and so in due time came back " to the said Prior of St. John." He told the Prior that he had better not touch the box, because it was very dangerous to those who were planning evil, and that if it even remained twenty-two hours in his house, that would be to his great danger. The Prior, thoroughly appalled, ordered Bernard to take the box, and go right away, and throw it somewhere where it would never be found. " And thus the said Bernard did, as he was commanded."

After which the Prior exhibited great anxiety to get Bernard out of the country. Bernard eventually consented to go, and came into Flanders where the more ordinary part of his report took place. In Flanders he saw letters from Perkin Warbeck to the Prior, signed " The Merchant of the Ruby " ; he knew merchants who conveyed them ; he heard of letters written to Thomas Brandon ; he knew the Prior wrote all his news from Flanders to the Bishop of Winchester, to John Hussey, to Sir Thomas Tyrrel, and to the Archdeacon ; he had heard Tyrrel and the Prior speak of " the son of King Edward," and wish him good will.

" Done at Rouen, the 14th day of March, in the year 1495 ; on the part of me, Bernard de Vignolles." And endorsed by the King.

Such was the tale. It is not perhaps likely that Henry believed it. But clearly M. de Vignolles thought he might.

At the court of the King of the Romans the Pretender was by this time pretending rather wildly. His two chief supporters were Maximilian and the Dowager Duchess ; he began to make promises in formal documents. He made Maximilian his heir to the English Throne, if he himself should die without issue ; he formally restored to Margaret the lands (including the town of Scarborough) and the revenues which Henry VII had seized and she still considered hers. He and Maximilian had something in common, a delight in invention and adventurous fables ;

it pleased them both to play with kingdoms after this manner. A verbal promise might have been reasonable ; to execute instruments was carrying the magnificent drama of dreams rather far. The drama in fact was interrupted by the active dreams of another monarch. The city chronicler far away in London wrote : " In this year the French king passed the mountains through Italy, and so to Rome ; and after into Naples with a great people, and constrained the King of Naples to flee from his country, and did many other great deeds. Also this year in Lent white herring was of such plenty in London, that after mid-Lent men might have bought a barrel of good herring of lawful assise for 3s. 4d. Also——" but it is the King of France that concerns us.

He had come down into Italy to claim Naples. In Florence Savonarola welcomed him ; the Pope fled to St. Angelo and saw the Frankish invaders camped by Rome. The unbroken success of the French king's progress alarmed the other courts of Europe, except the English. It became the purpose of those courts to involve the English, by alarm or otherwise, in the league that was being formed against France. It became a question among the diplomats whether this could best be achieved by suppressing Warbeck and supporting Henry or by supporting Warbeck and overthrowing Henry. At first it seemed most likely that the chances were in favour of Warbeck.

Maximilian entertained hopes that if the Pretender could obtain England he would attack France; he therefore assisted him as best he could. Henry found at last a real attack from Warbeck threatening. In July 1495 the ships of the Pretender appeared off Deal. The King's previous actions however had prevented any rising among the gentry, and the Kentish men were not anxious to join the rebels and foreign levies. "On Friday, 3rd July," wrote the Spanish ambassador, "the so-called Duke of York came to England. A portion of his troops disembarked, but the people rose in arms against them without the intervention of a single soldier of the King." "The Mayor of Sandwich," wrote the City chronicler, "with certain Commons of that county, to the number of seven or eight score, bickered with the residue [of the invaders] that were upon land and took alive of them a hundred and sixty-nine persons, and after the said discomfiture the said rebels within the said ships drew up their sails and sailed westward." The prisoners were brought to London and "in carts and long ropes" taken to the Tower. During the next two months they were tried and put to death. They were hanged in Kent and Essex, in Suffolk and Norfolk, "by the sea's side," at Wapping "in the water," and at Tyburn. Others of higher rank were beheaded in the Tower. One only of the mass escaped—while he was being carried down to suffer death in Essex; at Chelmsford he managed to get through the windows of a stable, and got away to sanctuary at Westminster. The rest dangled all along the south-eastern coasts, a warning to the country folk to beware how they supported rebels coming by sea.

The Pretender himself passed on to Ireland. It was probably in that connexion that the King had a census taken through the country of all Irish people dwelling in England—their names, ages, and faculties, as a guard against future dangers. Varying reports came to the Continent: on 17th July Maximilian was reporting to the Venetian ambassadors that the Duke of York " has reached England and been received by some of his adherents, whereat his Majesty rejoiced greatly, as he could dispose of the Duke of York *ad libitum suum.*" On 16th August the ambassadors were writing to their government that the King of the Romans was waiting the result of the expedition, " as, should he (Warbeck) succeed ... Maximilian would admit him ... whilst, should the Duke be worsted, the present King will be accepted in his stead." On 22nd August, Ferdinand and Isabella were writing that they were very glad to hear that " the person who calls himself Duke of York " had not invaded England. Henry was more free now to do what it becomes him to do; the Duke seems to have turned out an impostor.

What, in Ferdinand's eyes, it became Henry to do was immediately to join the League against France. Henry was determined first to extract an abandonment of Warbeck from Maximilian. Maximilian conceived his honour concerned; he would not yield. The Spanish sovereigns wrote explaining that Henry must not mind; that even if Maximilian would not accept Henry instead of Richard, Henry must not mind. " It would not be honest of the King of the Romans to declare himself against *him* whom he has kept at his court. It must be well understood that *we* will help the King of England against him of York." It seemed at first to the sovereigns that the best thing would be to get hold of the Pretender's person; but then, on the other hand, they could not well keep him and they certainly would not deliver him up to Henry. They hoped he had been already taken prisoner. But he had not; by then he was in Scotland. The attempt on Ireland had failed as the attempt on Kent had failed. But Scotland was another matter; James IV welcomed the Pretender heartily. Preparations for war were made, and preparations for love. James determined to marry the Duke to a lady of his court.

Henry meanwhile was meditating, if not love, at least another marriage. The Princess Margaret was unpledged; her father considered it was worth while buying James off with her hand.

James showed no eagerness for the marriage. He went on making ready for war. The Pretender was fortunate to find another royal believer in him, and one who was more happily situated for attacking England. The Scottish King was, of course, hampered by those of his nobles who, like the Lord Bothwell, were anxious to betray him to England. Henry had bought a number of the servants of the Scottish Throne. In proportion as James's preparations increased, the Spanish sovereigns grew almost flustered in their efforts to persuade Henry to join the League. They consented to their ambassador luring " him of York " into their own hands; they offered Henry any testimonials to his actual life they could supply; they attempted to drive or guide the King of the Romans into a reconciliation with Henry. "Concerning your wish that he of York were in our power," wrote Isabella to the ambassador, "you can assure the King of England that we will employ ourselves in the matter as in one that concerns ourselves." She had no belief in Warbeck's success. She judged well. But it may have been the subtle influence of Henry, working through De Puebla, that persuaded her.

But gradually Warbeck's claims were universally forgotten in the clamour for Henry's help. Both the French King and the Spanish offered to get hold of Warbeck's parents and send them to England; both sent envoys to Scotland who were instructed to try and purchase the Pretender's person from James. At Nordlingen on 6th January 1495/6 there was a kind of League of Nations—a meeting of all the ambassadors to Maximilian, to whom his representative announced his proposed demands on and reply to Henry's ambassador. The King of the Romans wished to say that " he considered it his duty not to abandon the Duke," but " should the King of England approve, the King of the Romans offered to negotiate a ten-years' peace between him and the Duke of York." The other ambassadors protested; the Spanish urged that such proposals would only irritate Henry, the Venetian said it was very desirable that the King of the Romans " should drop the affairs of the Duke of York " as it was not the moment to disturb the kingdom of England, the Neapolitan and Milanese warmly agreed. The Imperial representative withdrew and reported their opinions to his master. In that brief space the fate of the Merchant of the Ruby hung level. But the need of procuring the Tudor's support for the League against France was too urgent and too obvious. When the King's councillor returned to the assembled representatives he announced that his master was content " to cancel all the paragraphs relating to the Duke of York." It was the moment of the real decision of Europe in favour of the Tudors. It is true Maximilian still hankered after supporting Warbeck; and there was a good deal of diplomatic wrestling between him and Christopher Urswick who came riding into Augsburg at the end of April. But the rest of the Concert would not allow Maximilian to change. By July Henry had won. He deigned to accede to the League. The Duke of York disappeared from the councils of the League. The Pope published a brief of plenary absolution; proclamation of which and of the League was made at Rome and immediately printed with pictures of the contracting sovereigns and couplets describing them. The four of most interest were;

" This is Pope Alexander, who corrects
The errors of the world by laws divine.

Long life to the Cæsarean Emperor August,
King of the Romans, Maximilian the Just.

This is the great King of Spain and his Queen,
Who of the Infidels made havoc extreme."

And of Henry:

" This is that King who will yet cause consternation
To every foe of the firm confederation."[1]

In spite, however, of verses, pictures, printings, and absolutions, the King of England did not at once ratify the treaty. There was yet one quarter from which peace was not to be expected, one knight-errant who was preparing to charge in

[1] The translations are G. A. Bergenroth's.

support of the White Rose, and he was James of Scotland. Henry did not propose to leave Europe entirely at ease until he was himself entirely at ease. He wished that Europe should wish the knight-errant to keep quiet, which indeed it was by the mouths of the Pope and the King of Spain urging him to do. But the old enmity and the new loyalty in the heart of James Stuart were too strong for such international acquiescence, and precisely in the degree to which Perkin Warbeck lost in Augsburg he gained in Edinburgh. While Urswick was diplomatizing with Maximilian, James Stuart was making arms. While the King of the Romans was reluctantly dropping the Duke of York from his intimate concerns, the King of Scotland was admitting him to his intimate kinsfolk. The Pretender was married to Lady Katherine Gordon. There is in existence a letter which has been ascribed to Warbeck, and supposed to have been written to Lady Katherine. It has about it a rhetoric of love, and is perhaps rather a gesture of high manners than a profound admission of passion. Warbeck was then twenty-one or twenty-two. He had for five years been, justly or unjustly, playing the part of royalty, and playing it among royalties. He perhaps half-believed himself; who could know what strange adventures lay in the forgotten years of childhood? Many adolescents have sighed to discover some parentage greater than that they confess, sighed without finding it offered them. Warbeck had had it. He had carried that other reported parentage to the courts of France and Burgundy and Vienna ; he was dispossessed England—and now he was dispossessed England in love.

"Most noble lady, it is not without reason that all turn their eyes to you ; that all admire, love, and obey you. For they see your two-fold virtues by which you are so much distinguished above all other mortals. Whilst, on the one hand, they admire your riches and immutable prosperity, which secure to you the nobility of your lineage and the loftiness of your rank, they are, on the other hand, struck by your rather divine than human beauty, and believe that you are not born in our days, but descended from Heaven.

"All look at your face, so bright and serene that it gives splendour to the cloudy sky ; all look at your eyes as brilliant as stars, which make all pain to be forgotten, and turn despair into delight ; all look at your neck, which outshines pearls ; all look at your fine forehead, your purple light of youth, your fair hair ; in one word, at the splendid perfection of your person ; and looking at, they cannot choose but admire you ; admiring, they cannot choose but love you ; loving, they cannot choose but obey you.

"I shall, perhaps, be the happiest of all your admirers, and the happiest man on earth, since I have reason to hope you will think me worthy of your love. If I represent to my mind all your perfections, I am not only compelled to love, to adore, and to worship you, but love makes me your slave. Whether waking or sleeping, I cannot find rest or happiness except in your affection. All my hopes rest in you, and in you alone.

"Most noble lady, my soul, look mercifully down upon me your slave, who has ever been devoted to you from the first hour he saw you. Love is not an earthly thing, it is heaven-born. Do not think it below yourself to obey love's dictates. Not only kings, but also gods and goddesses have bent their necks beneath its yoke.

"I beseech you, most noble lady, to accept for ever one who in all things will cheerfully do your will as long as his days shall last. Farewell, my soul and my consolation. You, the brightest ornament of Scotland, farewell, farewell."

In July the Pretender lost his chance in the chief diplomacy abroad; in September he was offered a more direct chance in battle at home. James, carrying Warbeck with him, and issuing denunciations of one Henry Tydder, crossed the frontier. The report of the invasion given by the City chronicler (he was writing under the Mayoralty of Henry Colet, father of John Colet) describes the result as it was known in London, with a proper patriotic content:

"And this year in the month of September the king of Scots, with banner displayed, with great number of Scots entered four miles within this land, and burnt houses and cast down two small towers or piles, making great boast and brag. But when he understood of the Lord Neville's coming with four thousand men, and other of the March party coming after to have given him battle, at midnight after, he with his people departed in such haste that over the water of the Tweed, which in his coming in to this land he was two days in conveying, at his returning home he was, and all his people, set over in eight hours."

What appears to have happened is that the Pretender was shocked by the appearance of war. The burning houses, the ruined towers, the killing of villagers, all the usual accompaniments of a Border invasion on a large scale made his romance a dreadful reality. It was his people whom he saw the Scots host destroying, his not only by right but by his own decision. His pretence to royalty drove him further than a real royalty had driven Margaret of Anjou or Edward IV or even Henry Tudor himself. He protested to James. James, angry at the failure of the war, turned his discontent against his guest and client. In London Henry at last permitted himself to ratify the League. On 1st November there was a grand procession when the King went through St. Paul's. Before him were carried a sword and Cap of Maintenance received the previous day as a gift from the Pope. After the procession, Morton, now Cardinal-Archbishop of Canterbury, standing on the steps of the choir, delivered a sermon lasting almost an hour, " concerning the cause of the sending." He was by now an old man of seventy-six; he had four more years to live. He had seen the adventurer whom, twenty and more years before, he had himself proposed for the Crown, now united with the other kings of Europe to serve and defend the Papacy. The two chief causes of his life were fortunately conjoined. There was one other in which he half failed—it was the reformation of the Church, its purifying from abuses, its encouragement towards holiness. He was engaged on it; he was not to know that before he, or sincere souls after him, could carry it to its conclusion, it was to be thwarted by destruction, and another reformation taken in hand. He preached; that night there were fires of celebration of the Papal honour lit " in divers places of the City."

Six weeks later the Archbishop made another speech, this time in the Parliament. The King had already taken steps to raise money. Seven days before the ceremony at St. Paul's he had caused a special assembly to be held at Westminster—neither his ordinary council nor Parliament, but a gathering of spiritual and temporal peers, and representatives of the towns and the merchants. They were summoned to vote money, which they did: £120,000. With this agreement behind him Henry proceeded to raise forced loans from the rich. In January 1496/7 Parliament voted further grants. It is to be supposed that there was theoretically some relation between the two votes; in practice, however, it is doubtful if the King would not regard both of them as necessary payments made to the Crown. Both were for the Scottish war, which Henry proposed now to pursue on his own side. Men were ordered north, and preparations made in the north.

An unexpected war at that moment broke out in the south, in Cornwall. The attempt to gather in the taxes provoked a riot ; the riot proposed revolution. A huge mob, ordering itself in some half-disciplined way, led by a blacksmith, a lawyer, and a peer, put itself in movement first to Exeter, and then marched across southern England towards Kent. The purpose can only have been to gather strength, but it failed ; indeed when the rebels reached Kent they found the local levies in arms against them. They turned north towards London. By the middle of June they were at St. George's in the Fields, and some of them were already in touch with the officers of the King's army, offering to surrender their leaders in return for a pardon. On 16th June the rebels reached Blackheath. They were by now in a high state of division ; away from their homes, faced by the King's army, with only a choice of submission or battle. It is clear that those movements of the populace were not unlike our own hunger-marchers, with certain differences ; (i) they might be for other than economic causes : (ii) they were composed of men all of whom were used to carry and to use some kind of weapon. The explosive capacity of such men was often high. An expedition would set out towards the Throne, half as a demonstration, half as a threat. On its way it would become divided into two tendencies; those who wished to strengthen the threat, and those who wished to modify the demonstration. The marchers would encounter several odd bodies of local levies—as it were, of the county police—with whom they would deal as the time and their temper allowed. A man might be killed, or a house burnt. Near London they would come into hearing or sight of the regular troops, and be ordered to disperse. They would surge into a decision, but the result was the same. If the modifiers were in the majority, "the rebels fled"; if the threateners, "the rebels were crushed."

Such was the history of the Cornish rebellion now. Owing to the absence of his men in the north, Henry seems to have been taken by surprise; and most of his men were in the north, and he had to recall them. But he had not intended that the rebels should get so near London. He had meant them to be destroyed earlier, which, it was said, "The King's Grace had liever had been done than £20,000 for his honour." Cornish rebels at the gates of London looked bad abroad, especially if the peace and quietness of the future life of the Princess Katherine of Spain had to be favourably presented in Madrid. On the night before the battle the King himself was with his troops; he was now a man of forty, "abruing and comforting his people." On 17th June, at six in the morning, the King's men attacked; the rebels broke; and Henry, coming up in command of the rearguard, was free to ride over the whole field.

The rebellion had been ended. But it is not impossible that the rebellion had some effect in hastening the embassy that Henry now sent into Scotland. Another of the diplomatic body, Richard Fox, now Bishop of Durham, was sent to try and arrange terms of peace. He set out on 4th July 1497, the remote precursor, as Bacon pointed out, of that faster ride which Sir Robert Carew was to take one hundred and six years afterwards, bearing the news of the death of Elizabeth. Fox, was above all, to demand the surrender of Warbeck. His instructions carry Henry's trick of assuming his own prestige and exhibiting a slight contempt for his enemies. The Pretender must be given up; "Not for any estimation that we take of him," but because it was on his behalf that the invasion by James had taken place, " and less, therefore, may we not do with our honour than to have the deliverance of him, though the deliverance or having of him is of no price nor value."

Henry, however, would not insist even on this. If Fox could not get it, he was to take less, he was to take what he could, he was (in the last resort) to take what James would offer. Fortunately, however, both he and James were enabled to retain their separate exactitudes of honour; Henry in demanding, James in denying, the surrender. For Warbeck was not there. He had left—perhaps he had to leave—Scotland; he had departed almost before Fox had started. James did not exactly abandon Warbeck, but he apparently encouraged Warbeck to abandon James. He gave him two or three ships, with some men. Katherine Gordon accompanied her husband. There are all the signs of a permanent but polite break. It is true that James then proceeded to attack England again, in August, and laid siege on the castle of Norham, on the Tweed. Perkin may have been meant to raise his standard in the south while James attacked from the north. But as he did not go to England for some weeks, it looks as if the arrangement was loose. James had abandoned knight-errantry on the Pretender's behalf; he left him to make what he could as he could, while remaining aware that his own acts might give him a better chance than he could otherwise have.

The three small vessels, beating down from Scotland, carry a kind of doubly forlorn hope. The figures of the rash young romantic and his wife are forlorn not only in their present but with our knowledge that their future is already pathetically defeated. They come to Ireland; the Pretender disembarks: he finds conditions heavily changed. The Earl of Desmond and the Earl of Kildare try now to catch him; his single serious adherent is killed. He puts to sea again. The ship by misadventure finds itself among King Henry's fleet; it is stopped, and boarded. The commander of the fleet offers the captain and crew two thousand nobles to give up Warbeck, if they have him. The crew—they were Biscayans —swear that they never knew or heard of such a man. Below them, while they swear, hidden in a pipe of wine, lies the Pretender. The defeated English retire; the single ship hurries on. He has escaped to land at last, to land in England—near Land's End.

There are about a hundred men with him. Now it has come to it, now he is in his own country, he lets his pretence or his fate rise to its height. He proclaims himself as Richard IV, King of England; the discontented or riotous— "most part naked men"—who joins him give him a following of some three thousand. He moves on to Bodmin; to Exeter from which he is beaten off; to Taunton. The ordered armies of King Henry begin to occupy the West of England, King Henry himself commanding the rearguard. On the night of the 20th September, King Richard fled. It may have been doubt or despair; it may also have been a renewal of that pity and horror with which in the North he had seen the Scots destroying his people. He rode to the Abbey at Beaulieu, and took sanctuary. His army—to call it that—surrendered to King Henry, whose troops took the ringleaders prisoner, and surrounded the chief leader in his place of retreat. He was accompanied by three of his friends, or (as the loyalists mockingly said) of his Council. They waited a week; they gave themselves up. King Richard was carried before King Henry at Taunton. His wife, found and seized at St. Michael's Mount, was brought to meet him before King Henry at Exeter.

The act of royalty was done. Before the Tudor, in the presence of Katherine Gordon, among the court of England, the Flemish boatman's son told his story—" an alien of no ability by his poor parents." He was pardoned; the real business forgave the false dream for existing. Presently he was brought to London, and there paraded about the streets, with one of his followers, who had formerly been in King Henry's service, after him. This man was put to death, but Warbeck was held in custody at Westminster. It was 28th December 1497.

On 6th December at Leadenhall and so afterwards through the City there was another show. The King's heralds proclaimed a peace between the Kings of England and Scotland—" for the term of both their lives and either of them longest living, and a year after." It was the preliminary to the real future of the Throne of England.

CHAPTER VI

THE MARRIAGES

(i)

THE Milanese ambassador, writing to Ludovic Sforza, Duke of Milan, on 8th September 1497, discussed King Henry at some length. He was struck first by the amount of accurate information the King had on European affairs. It was derived from various sources—from his own representatives, from the subjects of other countries whom the King had in his pay, and from the merchants, and as a result Henry was so well informed that if the Duke wished to send any news, the ambassador wrote, it would be well either to give it in special detail or before others could convey it. The letter of congratulation which the Duke had sent on the King's July victories against the Cornishmen and the Scots "is to the purpose though rather late." Henry had made no brag; talking to the ambassador of the northern invasion, he was more moderate than the City Chronicler. He said only that the King of Scotland had raised his camp "not very gloriously," and about Warbeck he said nothing whatever. Nor, it seems, was Henry the kind of person one could ask what had happened to the Pretender. "He kept state and majesty to the height," wrote Bacon, and again; "he put them into admiration to find his universal insight into the affairs of the world."

The Milanese, a little abashed by the King's highness, was left to hear from others that Warbeck had disappeared from Scotland; "so I consider that this youth called Perkin has vanished into smoke."

He suggested that the Duke should congratulate the Spanish sovereigns on their proposed son-in-law Arthur. The dynasty would be established by that marriage, though the kingdom was perfectly stable, which was due, first, to the King's wisdom "whereof everyone stands in awe," and, secondly, to the King's wealth—"his revenue is great and real, not lying merely in documents." It was these two points which struck foreign visitors. "Wisdom" there is, of course, political wisdom, statecraft, diplomacy, cunning. Dr. De Puebla was continually implying it, but that went for little. A newly arrived Venetian ambassador, also in 1497, after a two-hour audience with Henry, wrote: "The King is gracious and grave, and a very wealthy person." The accidents of Henry's success, reign, and royalty, were giving place to his more essential character as the thing to be considered. His character, it is to be feared, was measured by his worldly triumph; though certainly Henry was favoured by heaven—heaven at least in the shape of Alexander VI. " The Pope," the Milanese continued, " is entitled to much praise, for he loves the King cordially and strengthens his power by ecclesiastical censures, so that at all times rebels are excommunicated. The efficacy of these censures is now felt by the Cornishmen, for all who eat grain garnered since the rebellion, or drink beer brewed with this year's crop, die as if they had taken poison and hence it is publicly reported that the King is under the protection of God eternal." It seems, from that sentence, as if Alexander VI, if not God, might have said to Henry : " Behold, I have cursed the earth for thy sake."

Even the Spanish sovereigns changed their tune. The old marriage treaty had been dropped when Henry had become friendly with France after his gaudy war, and at some time about then the signature of Ferdinand and Isabella had been cut away from the original treaty, which they, though not Henry, had ratified. But when Henry was to be beguiled or threatened into joining the League, the marriage idea was revived. At first it was made conditional on Henry being reconciled to Maximilian ; and the tone of Spanish diplomacy was high. As the weeks slipped by, and Henry (with some reason) went on talking about Maximilian's support of the Pretender, the note of the letters was abated. In 1496 Ferdinand and Isabella were instructing De Puebla that he was to try to content the King of England with a marriage dowry of one hundred thousand doubloons; if he failed, the dowry was to be kept as small as possible. The rate of exchange was to be one English crown against 328 maravedis; if the King would not be content, De Puebla might rise to 350 maravedis. The urgency, the ambassador was told, was great. Even when Henry had joined the League, his admirable passivity continued to fret his allies. He had not declared, nor did he seem likely to declare, war against France. Isabella wrote again and again to De Puebla. She said they would defend England " against anyone whatever," but that this willingness had better be concealed from the King of the Romans and the Pope. She insisted that Henry's adherence to the League should be proclaimed, but that any clauses unfavourable to the allies should be kept secret. She ordered him to be told that she thought him " a Prince of great virtue, firmness, and constancy." She had a great love for him; she hoped—after the marriage—they would be more intimate than any other princes. If he would not declare war, which would " put the finishing-stroke to a thing of immense and universal good," at least he could assist Spain by sea. He must be able to do *something*.

The marriage treaty was signed and ratified. Henry wrote to Ferdinand and Isabella. He professed a love even more intimate and sincere than Isabella's : " neither letters nor signs could express it." But after the marriage (he said) he should be even more affectionate. He turned to De Puebla, who had (one may suppose) been of considerable use to him in conveying to Spain the extreme views of the King of England's resources, independence, and capacious diplomacy. He had heard, Henry wrote, that De Puebla had " been reproached for remissness." In fact, however, no ambassador had ever been so " industrious, vigilant, true, and adroit," and he deserved some signal reward. This was on 14th December 1497. In the following February, no reward having arrived, Henry wrote again. He wished to offer De Puebla a bishopric, but De Puebla had refused to accept it : the King and Queen of England had therefore persuaded him to accept " an honourable marriage." But he would only agree even to this if his own sovereign assented. Henry therefore begged them to grant his and his Queen's request. A month later the sovereigns, far from doing anything of the kind, were writing to their envoy to Flanders, Londoño, who was to spend some time in England on the way, that he was to inquire how De Puebla had been conducting his business. " It is said he is entirely in the interests of King Henry."

It was, at the moment, peculiarly difficult for De Puebla since he was already on very bad terms with another Spanish gentleman, the Don Pedro de Ayala, who had been ambassador to Scotland and had now been in England for some six months. The two were entirely antipathetic. " He is causing me," wrote De Puebla, " incredible trouble." There had been fighting between Don Pedro's servants and the English; one of his servants had been arrested, and would have been hanged, " if the King had not interceded." There were thus, at that time, three Spanish representatives in England; each writing about the others. It must be admitted that De Puebla was not much admired by either of the others, and it was at this point that the criticism of him became vocal.

It is clear that Henry was managing De Puebla by an impassioned presentation of his own feeling for Spain, and that De Puebla accepted this partly because of Henry's exhibition of his feeling for him. When Londoño and his colleagues arrived in London they were given an audience. Of the King's speech and of Morton's, Londoño wrote : " King Henry gave a very gracious and satisfactory answer with a most cheerful countenance. The Cardinal afterwards made a speech . . . and answered every point of their message." But De Puebla wrote : " The speeches of the King in French and the Cardinal in Latin were remarkably fine. They could not have been better. I did not speak that day except sometimes to explain a little in detail." On the next day, however, while Londoño rested, and made inquiries about De Puebla, and probably talked with Ayala, De Puebla himself was at the Palace, holding private conversations. The King told him that he had enjoyed the letters which Londoño brought more than his late victory over Warbeck; he could not have them read often enough. He detained De Puebla for a long conversation, at which his mother and his wife were present. The three appear to have indulged in what was almost a leg-pulling competition. " To hear what they spoke of Your Highnesses and of the Princess of Wales was like hearing the praise of God." " The King had a dispute with the Queen because he wanted to have one of the said letters to carry about with him continually, but the Queen did not like to part with hers, having sent the other to the Prince of Wales."

No doubt Henry was pleased to see the marriage taking shape. But the picture of him—he the watchful, the careful, the considerate, ever ready with alternatives, ever just not giving the last penny—romantically carrying about with him the letter of that other King with whom he had for ten years been negotiating and arguing, whom he had virtually cheated, and by whom he had virtually been cheated; the picture of him tearing, as it were, from his wife's hands the precious signature of Ferdinand and Isabella that he might treasure them in secret—no. No one but De Puebla thought so. Londoño admitted that the King spoke in words which showed "great love and affection," but there he stopped. "King Henry said that he is very well satisfied with De Puebla . . . that no other ambassador could conduct the negotiations as well as he does, adding, that he makes these observations only to recommend De Puebla to his masters. We suspect, however, that De Puebla has begged the King to speak of him in that way . . . King Henry is certainly satisfied with De Puebla because he carries on negotiations rather in the interest of England than of Spain." Londoño proceeded to give examples—matters of trade, and again the matter of the marriage. "Henry was in the midst of his difficulties with Scotland and Perkin. . . . If any other man had been ambassador, their Highnesses would have dictated conditions to England. The King would have given much money besides." It was too late. Henry had his treaty, but he had not made war on France. "He is rich, has established good order in England, and keeps the people in such subjection as has never been the case before. . . . He is a friend of peace.'"

Such, to the new eyes of the foreign embassy, were the two men by whom the great episode of Katherine of Aragon was opened; such especially was their own countryman. Deformed, greedy,

THE MARRIAGES 147

foolish, mocked almost openly by the King's mother and by the Queen, mildly dispraised even by Henry to others, and yet the important man through those critical months, De Puebla welcomes the ships of his sovereign's daughter into England—and prepares, nearly a century later, the reign of Elizabeth and those other ships of the Armada.

The view which Ayala took of Henry may as well be recorded here, because it begins to anticipate the future Henry in the eleven years that remained rather than to be an altogether accurate description of the past.

" The King of England is less rich than is generally said. He likes to be thought very rich, because such a belief is advantageous to him in many respects. His revenues are considerable, but the custom house revenues, as well as the land rents, diminish every day. As far as the customs are concerned, the reason of their decrease is to be sought in the decay of commerce, caused partly by the wars, but much more by the additional duties imposed by the King. There is, however, another reason for the decrease of trade, that is to say, the impoverishment of the people by the great taxes laid on them. The King himself said to me, that it is his intention to keep his subjects low, because riches would only make them haughty. The rents of the domains which he has confiscated to the Crown have much diminished.

" His crown is, nevertheless, undisputed, and his government is strong in all respects. He is disliked, but the Queen beloved, because she is powerless. They love the Prince as much as themselves, because he is the grandchild of his grandfather. Those who know him love him also for his own virtues. The King looks old for his years, but young for the sorrowful life he has led. One of the reasons why he leads a good life is that he has been brought up abroad. He would like to govern England in the French fashion, but he cannot. He is subject to his Council, but has already shaken off some, and got rid of some part of this subjection. Those who have received the greatest favours from him are the most discontented. He knows all that. The King has the greatest desire to employ foreigners in his service. He cannot do so; for the envy of the English is diabolical, and, I think, without equal. He likes to be much spoken of, and to be highly appreciated by the whole world. He fails in this, because he is not a great man. Although he professes many virtues, his love of money is too great.

"He spends all the time he is not in public, or in his Council, in writing the accounts of his expenses with his own hand. He desires nothing more in this world than the arrival of the Princess of Wales in England. Though it is not my business to give advice, I take the liberty to say that it would be a good thing if she were to come soon, in order to accustom herself to the way of life in this country and to learn the language. On the other hand, when one sees and knows the manners and the way of life of this people in this island, one cannot deny the grave inconveniences of her coming to England before she is of age. Your Highnesses know the reasons. They are many. But the Princess can only be expected to lead a happy life through not remembering those things which would make her less enjoy what she will

THE MARRIAGES 149

find here. It would, therefore, still be best to send her directly, and before she has learnt fully to appreciate our habits of life and our government.

"The King is much influenced by his mother and his followers in affairs of personal interest and in others. The Queen, as is generally the case, does not like it."

In that last paragraph it seems unlikely that Ayala was right.

All this took place in July 1498. But in June the King had been shaken. It was almost a year since Perkin Warbeck had been taken, and he was still kept in a kind of custody about the court. Simnel had been quiet enough since he had been put in his place, and it was to be expected that Warbeck would be docile also. It is at least a half-argument in favour of Henry's own belief in Perkin's falsity that he should have been allowed so much liberty. The undoubted Earl of Warwick was kept more safely in the Tower. Yet the clemency shown by Henry exhibits a curious shadow. In June, De Puebla wrote: "I wrote a long time ago to your Highnesses, supplicating you to give your opinion and advice as to how the King of England ought to deal with Warbeck. Your Highnesses have not to this day, no doubt from some just reason and impediments, sent a word in reply or written anything. . . . Your silence causes much pain to me, because I am sure the King of England would do what your Highnesses might advise." This is not quite so certain as De Puebla thought, but the statement of his belief is of some interest. Henry had discussed something. The complaint was wrung from the ambassador by the next episode in the tale. " The said Perkin fled a few days ago, without any reason." Warbeck had revolted against the polished captivity, and had escaped. At first he tried to go to the coast ; he failed, for Henry had flung his watchers about the roads, and the fugitive was driven at last to take refuge in the monastery at Sheen, where the King had one of his favourite houses. He was surrendered to Henry, who sent immediate word of the recovery to De Puebla. " God be thanked ! Perkin is already captured," wrote the ambassador. " The same hour that he was arrested the King of England sent one of his gentlemen of the bed-chamber to tell me the news. . . . I think he will either be executed or kept with great vigilance in prison."

Either because his life had been promised to the prior of Sheen and Henry was punctilious in his religious observances, or because a mere effort at escape was not an obviously sufficient reason for death, he was not at the moment executed. He was kept, certainly " with great vigilance," in prison. He was plunged into a cell " where he sees neither sun nor moon," and only occasionally brought out to confirm his tale of deception. De Puebla wrote again, towards the end of August: "I saw how much altered Perkin was. He is so much changed that I, and all other persons here, believe his life will be very short. He must pay for what he has done." But deaths in prison are unsatisfactory. The Princes in the Tower, if Perkin were not one of them, had died so, and Perkin had been able to pretend to be one of them. Henry VII had something of the preference of Henry VIII for making his acts legal. There seems no doubt that he had been jarred by the escape—unless, indeed, a darker story than we know lies behind the escape. Henry's spies could always become agents provocateurs on occasion. But it is not fair to impute an extra occasion, in spite of the report that went to Venice: "The King arranged with some of Perkin's attendants that they should suggest to Perkin to escape out of his Majesty's hands; and thus did the youth do: so the King had him put in prison, where he will end his days." It is certain that after his execution De Puebla sent a pæan of delight to Ferdinand. There remained somewhere till then an element of uncertainty, and its pseudonym was Richard, Duke of York.

The King determined to remove it. At the beginning of 1499 another plot broke in Kent—another personification. The son of a cordwainer, who was the pupil of an Augustinian friar, set out and set up to be the Earl of Warwick.

It was the silliest of all the plots, for Kent was near London and Warwick was a prisoner in London. It failed. The lad—he was nineteen—was brought to London, to St. Thomas Watering, and there hanged. The body hung in its shirt " from the said Tuesday till the Saturday night again next following." He had lived at the Bull in Bishopsgate Street; his friends and acquaintances could take advice. For the first recorded time, the King was fretted. He had a priest, who had the gift of prophecy, brought to him; who was said to have foretold the deaths of King Edward and King Richard. Henry found little comfort in him; he only heard that his life would be in danger the whole year, and that there were " two parties, of very different political creeds, in the land." Dismissed, the priest chattered. He told a friend, who told a friend, and the second friend found himself in prison, but the others fled.

" Henry has aged so much during the last two weeks that he seems to be twenty years older." It is Ayala writing in March. He grew more devout. He heard a sermon every day during Lent. Something was on his mind about the past —or about the future, the November of that year. On the sixteenth of that month Warbeck was arraigned " in the White Hall at Westminster," with others, for certain treasons committed by them; on the nineteenth the Earl of Warwick was arraigned in the same place for the same cause.

The evidence depended mostly on an informer who was afterwards pardoned. To be fair, we cannot trace that he was rewarded as Clifford was rewarded; had he been, that would have been certain which is now all but certain. He had been in the Tower during August. The evidence given was that there had been concocted a plot between Warwick, Warbeck, the informer Claymound, and others, by which the Earl was to seize on the Tower and the Jewel House, fire the gunpowder, issue a proclamation calling for adherents, escape beyond seas, and finally—then or afterwards—depose and kill the King. He was to make himself king, and Warbeck (apparently) Governor. In the process of concocting this plot, Warwick had given Claymound a cloak and a jacket and he had sent presents to others. More astonishingly, he had got into communication with Warbeck, who was in the cell beneath, (a) by knocking on the floor and calling to him; (b) by sending documents to him through Claymound; (c) by making a hole in the stone floor of his cell and calling to him to be of good cheer. This last fantastic detail dances on the top of the whole episode, released from Claymound's tongue. Whether it were believed or not, it was certainly believed that there had been communication and a conspiracy to dethrone the King. The prisoners

—there were ten altogether—were found guilty ; one of the other eight was John Walter, once Mayor of Cork, who had been a supporter of Warbeck in Ireland. Four of them were executed ; the others were pardoned. Two of those put to death were Walter, and a man named Astwood, also a follower of Warbeck. The third was Warbeck himself. The fourth was Edward, Earl of Warwick, son of George, Duke of Clarence, son of Richard, Duke of York, and so to Edward III.

Perkin Warbeck was put to death at Tyburn, drawn there on a hurdle from the Tower, on St. Clement's Day, Saturday, 23rd November, a week after his arraignment. He confessed everything on the " small scaffold " : the confession was printed and circulated. On the next Thursday, 28th November, the Earl of Warwick was beheaded at the Tower, between two and three in the afternoon. He was twenty-one years old ; he had been in the Tower since 1485, when he was seven. This was the complete story of the boyhood, youth, and death of the last of the Plantagenets.

Some seven weeks afterwards De Puebla wrote to the Spanish sovereigns : " Most high and most powerful princes, the King and the Queen, Señores. After kissing the royal feet and the hands of your highnesses, I have to let you know that, by the fortune of your highnesses and the señora the

Princess of Wales, this kingdom is so disposed as has not been known for five hundred years, or so the learned say, and so the chronicles reveal; for there were always brambles and thorns to prevent the English remaining obedient to their king, the claimants to the kingdom being such that the quarrel could be maintained on both sides. Now God has seen fit that all should be completely purged and cleaned, in such a manner that not one drop of blood of doubtful royalty remains in the kingdom, but only the true blood of the King, the Queen, and especially of the señor the Prince Arthur; and since I have written to your highnesses in various ways of the justice done upon Perkin and on the son of the Duke of Clarence, I will not now importune you further with much writing."

The letters in which the ambassador had written of the " justice " done upon the son of the Duke of Clarence do not remain. There is, however, one, written on 5th October 1499, in which the señor the Prince Arthur had written to his bride—already pledged to him by several ceremonies of proxy marriages and ratifications of them by all the Princes—lamenting her delay and begging letters from her. It was not, however, till 2nd October 1501, almost two years after Warwick's execution, that the ship (built in the eclipse and rigged with curses dark) bearing the Princess Katherine at last entered Plymouth. The delay had been caused, partly by Ferdinand's suspicion that Henry was insincere in his proposals, partly by the effort to get Henry to agree that Katherine's own jewels were to be reckoned as part of her dowry. After that, she had started once, and been compelled to put back by storms. Her voyage over was accompanied by thunder storms, "every four or five hours. It was impossible not to be frightened." The comment is by one of her company, who added, concerning her arrival : " She could not have been received with greater rejoicings, if she had been the Saviour of the world." She met Henry and Arthur on the 6th November. Henry wrote to Ferdinand how much he admired her, and Arthur that he had never known so much joy as when he saw her sweet face. On 12th November she entered London over London Bridge, and was welcomed with decorations, triumphs, and pageants. Thomas More, a young man of twenty-three, then living with the monks of the Charterhouse, and studying at once devotion there, and law at Lincoln's Inn, watched the entry and admired the Princess, praying that the marriage might be "fortunate and of good omen." The most notable of the persons in the pageant, was perhaps God the Father (as was fitting for one who had excited joy equal to that caused by the Saviour of the world). He appeared in Chepe, in a heaven of seven candlesticks of gold, with wax candles burning in them; arranged outside the house of one William Geffrey, haberdasher. In the house were King Henry, the Queen, and others, watching the pageant. In view of what was to come, the poem recited by God the Father is of peculiar interest:

" I am beginning and end, that made each creature
Myself and for myself, but man specially,
Both male and female, made after mine own figure;
Whom I joined together in matrimony,
And that in Paradise, declaring openly
That men shall wedding in my church solemnize
Figured and signified by the earthly paradise.

In this my Church I am always resident,
As my chief Tabernacle and most chosen place,
Among these golden candlesticks, which represent
My Catholic Church, shining afore my face
With light of faith, wisdom, doctrine, and grace;
And marvellously eke inflamed toward me
With the inextinguible fire of Charity.

Wherefore my well-beloved daughter, Katherine,
Sith I have made you to my own Semblance
In my Church to be married, and your noble children
To reign in this land as in their inheritance,
See that ye have me in special remembrance;
Love me and my Church, your spiritual mother;
For ye despising that one despise that other.

Look that you walk my precepts, and obey them well,
And here I give you that same blessing that I
Gave my well-beloved Children of Israel:
Blessed be the fruit of your belly,
Your substance and fruits I shall increase and multiply,
Your rebellious enemies I shall put in your hand,
Increasing in honour both you and your land."

The marriage took place on Sunday, 14th November, at St. Paul's. The new Archbishop of Canterbury, Henry Deane, celebrated it; Morton had died in 1500. "Wonderful it was to behold the riches of garments and chains of gold that that day were worn by lords, knights, and gentlemen." The glories of the event proceeded for days, until at last the bride and bridegroom set out for the Prince of Wales' seat at Ludlow.

In less than five months all the long negotiations, all the splendid pageants, had come to nothing. Arthur was dead. The news came to King Henry.

"Immediately after his death Sir Richard Poole his Chamberlain, with other of his Council, wrote and sent letters to the King and Council to Greenwich, where his Grace and the Queen lay, and certified them of the Prince's departure. The which Council discreetly sent for the King's ghostly father a Friar Observant, to whom they shewed this most sorrowful and heavy tidings, and desired him in his best manner to show it to the King. He in the morning of the Tuesday following, somewhat before the time accustomed, knocked at the King's chamber door; and when the King understood it was his Confessor, he commanded to let him in. The Confessor then commanded all those there present to avoid, and after due salutation began to say, *Si bona de manu dei suscipimus, mala autem quare non sustineamus?* And so shewed his Grace that his dearest son was departed to God. When his Grace understood that sorrowful heavy tidings, he sent for the Queen, saying, that he and his Queen would take the painful sorrow together. After that she was come and saw the King her lord, and that natural and painful sorrow, as I have heard say, she with full great and constant comfortable words besought his Grace, that he would first, after God, remember the weal of his own noble person, the comfort of his realm, and of her. She then said, that my Lady his Mother had never no more children but him only, and that God by his grace had ever preserved him, and brought him where that he was. Over that, how that God had left him yet a fair Prince, two fair Princesses ; and that God is where he was, and that we are both young enough : And that the prudence and wisdom of his Grace sprung over all Christendom, so that it should please him to take this accordingly thereunto. Then the King thanked her of her good comfort. After that she was departed and come to her own chamber, natural and motherly remembrance of that great loss smote her so sorrowful to the heart, that those that were about her were fain to send for the King to comfort her. Then his Grace of true gentle and faithful love, in good haste came and relieved her, and showed her how wise council she had given him before ; and he for his part would thank God for his son, and would she do in like wise."

ii

Since the beginning of the reign the King had taken care to establish and increase his own party in Scotland. There was nothing unusual in this ; it was the habit of policy at the time. It was once said of Henry's own Council that most of them were in the pay of France, and though it seems not to have been true, it would not have surprised anyone. The difference between that age and this undoubtedly lies very largely in the matter of money. A minister in our day may reasonably pursue a policy favourable to some foreign government; he has not been, till recently, supposed to be in private communication with that government; still less has he been supposed to be in receipt of a private income from that government. When Europe is divided, as in the days of the Reformation and as in our own time, by great conflicting ideas, it is inevitable that such communications will exist. If England should ever be split into two parties, one of which was in strong sympathy with Moscow and one with Rome, it is pretty certain that the leaders of both sides would be in touch with sympathetic governments abroad. The question of taking money becomes then a matter of integrity and of discretion. Money may easily be sent to support a cause, and then to support persons useful to the cause. Other persons less useful, or perhaps not at all useful, will then tend to make themselves useful for the sake of the money. And future ages will denounce them.

The peculiarity of the age of Henry was that there were no principles at war, though there were preferences. Even the support given to the various claimants and Pretenders was in most cases a support designed for dynastic profit. The King of England was as willing as any other monarch to hire the nobles of other countries to serve him in their native lands. The difference between him and other monarchs was that he presently had much money to do the hiring and they had not so much. Ferdinand and Isabella contented themselves with writing letters to friendly English lords—to Buckingham, Suffolk, Surrey, Essex, and others, thanking them and urging them to go on being useful; Ferdinand in 1506 was paying at least six pensions of a thousand gold ducats a year for life to officers of the Courts of the Archduke Philip and the King of the Romans. The Bishop of London wrote to the sovereigns thanking them for the honour of their letter, and promising to do any service he could. None of them need imply what is called disloyalty. But they did imply a possible private relationship.

Henry's private relationship with the Scottish lords passed beyond such simple exchanges. He secretly hired the Earl of Angus, so that, in certain circumstances, Angus might make war on James. He secretly hired Patrick, the first Earl of Bothwell (great-grandfather of the most famous of the line), with even greater effect. Bothwell flung himself enthusiastically into Henry's interests. He laid plots to abduct James. He involved other lords in his " understanding" with the King of England. He reported to Henry all James's arrangements for the invasion of England. He urged Henry to be more warlike than the King had any intention of being. He offered suggestions on the burning of towns, the destruction of ships, and the cutting off of the invading army. But Henry was not anxious to arouse the last and most furious patriotism of the north. He was content to let James retire. He went on raising levies and preparing ships. De Puebla was instructed by the Spanish soverigns to moderate the King's wrath and modify his actions. He was to remember that the number of soldiers was not everything. "The stronger one is, the more must one justify one's cause and have God on one's side, as he may see from our example. . . . It seems to us he ought not to let slip this opportunity of arranging his affairs. The ill-advised affray in England must be forgotten."

Henry went on remembering it long enough to keep the Spanish ambassadors—De Puebla in England and Ayala in Scotland—anxious. They, with the League still in question, were unwilling that Henry should waste on Scotland the war preparations which would be much better directed against France. The King's troops remained mobilized in the north, and in June they even began to move forward. But the Cornish rebellion intervened. Fox's embassy, its rejection, and James's second raid followed. The negotiations were renewed, and the proclamation of peace followed. All this was but a preliminary; the real aim was the marriage of James to the Princess Margaret. The Spanish influence was on the side of the match, but James was apathetic and Henry was diplomatic. Ayala wrote that James was so against the marriage, because Margaret was only nine, and that a better way of maintaining a peace would be to marry James to a Spanish princess. "The English wish for this match, but, on the other hand, they are jealous and dislike the idea of the Scotch having the same honour as they have. The King alone, as being more intelligent, and not a pure Englishman, does not share this jealousy."

James was understood to have expressed a willingness to wait a few years for Margaret. It was understood he had consolations. Even the Spanish sovereigns could not make out quite what he wanted: "Does he wish to marry our daughter or our niece? or is he reconciled with England?" By 1500, however, the antipathetic James and Henry had drifted into a kind of mutual recognition that the marriage should take place. Presently an embassy came from Scotland; and arrived at Bishopsgate on the Saturday following Katherine's wedding, the twentieth of

November. Bothwell was one member of it; another was William Dunbar, in attendance on the Archbishop of Glasgow. In the Christmas week of 1501 " the Mayor had to dinner the ambassadors of Scotland, whom accompanied my lord Chancellor and other lords of this realm : where sitting at dinner one of the said Scots giving attendance upon a bishop, ambassador, the which was reported to be a protonotary of Scotland and servant of the said bishop, made this ballad following :

> London, thou art of Townes *a per se*,
> Sovereign of Cities, seemliest in sight. . . .

And so, according to the *City Chronicle*, through the complete poem. It was a pleasant prelude to the marriage. On 31st December " the Rhymer of Scotland " is stated in the King's accounts to have received £6 13s. 4d. and again on 7th January 1501/2 ; which might come to about two hundred pounds of our money— almost the equivalent of the traditional " purse of gold." But Dunbar was also writing a less known and less good poem called " The Thistle and the Rose," in celebration of the marriage. It was probably that for which the King rewarded him ; Henry would hardly have thought London worth so much.

On 25th January following proclamation of the marriage was made at Paul's Cross, and a

Te Deum sung. The usual bonfires were lit in the evening, and a hogshead of wine broached at every fire, "the which in time of the fire's burning was drunken of such as would, the which wine was not long in drinking."

CHAPTER VII

THE KING IN HIS STATE

IT is part of the fantasy of Henry VII that he lived in the grand opening of the Renascence. Had he been audible and visible, we should have seen more clearly than we now can an English figure in whom two ages were composed. Henry VI who died fourteen years after the Tudor's birth is almost pure medieval; Henry VIII who was born eighteen years before his death is almost pure Renascence. It might, of course, be held that Henry VII expressed the superstitions of both, if not their vices, and there is a good deal to be said for that point of view. He had something of the narrower piety of the Middle Ages and something of the more domestic gorgeousness of the Renascence. He avoided the *coups-de-théâtre* of both; in that he was more like the nineteenth century.

But if he were not theatrical by nature, he yet treated himself as a figure of the theatre of the time. He wore magnificent clothes, superb jewels, and the rich and glittering collars which were a characteristic of the age. He displayed himself so to the foreign ambassadors. He moved in public under a canopy of state, and as much of ceremonial as could be arranged went around him. He was served by nobles, and more than a thousand pounds a month went to supply the tables at which something like seven hundred persons dined. There were shows and tournaments and dances. There were leopards in the Tower and jesters in the Court. There were minstrels and huntsmen—and Henry seems to have had a liking for music and a liking for hunting. Yet with all this splendour there lingers that view of him of which Bacon knew the tradition: "For his pleasures there is no news of them." One would think there was a good deal. But they are like the frankness of which the ambassadors sometimes spoke; they do not altogether convince. Somewhere surely, if he took delight, there would be a single tale of a particular preference, an anecdote, a phrase. There is none. It is always the King without a face, the motionless wax adorned with flickering jewels. Or if there is anything more, it is but a suggestion that Bacon's further description was true: when he wrote how in all his leisure the King made notes—" especially touching persons," whom to employ, whom to reward or to watch, who followed whom or went with whom, charting the Court in which he moved like the ship of John Cabot among the dangers of the northern seas.

It is true he was unfortunate. He was very willing to behave as a King should, to encourage culture and to reward genius. Culture, however, —that is, the New Learning, and all that it meant—was only just reaching England, and of genius the age was singularly devoid. He paid money to poets, but the poets are largely lost to us. Hampton of Worcester in 1495 had one pound for making of ballads. In 1496 "an Italian, a poet," received twenty pounds. The blind poet, Bernard Andreas, received various rewards, an annuity, and was called by the title of Laureate. The Rhymer of Scotland, on the last day of 1502, received £6, 13s. 4d.; it was probably Dunbar. Master Peter, the poet, who may have been also the Italian poet, received rewards. Unfortunately none of them matter much. Elizabeth, for probably less expenditure, was "escorted down the years." Her grandfather had to put up with Andreas and Hampton of Worcester; and his reputation stopped at his death. There was certainly Skelton, who was appointed tutor to the Prince Henry. The King's ill-luck, however, pursued him even there; it was not until the end of the reign that Skelton began to write really Skeltonian poems. Up till then he was almost courtly.

In effect, original poetic energy hardly existed in England. Perhaps the finest poem written during the reign was the Lament by the young Thomas More on the death of the Queen in 1503. It is a little long to give here, but because it is not so well known as it should be, and because it is lovely, and because More imagined the whole of that royal house, and because of the future, the liberty may be taken. After all, there is no rival; we cannot do anything like it again. More was twenty-five at the time.

> " O ye that put your trust and confidence
> In worldly joy and frail prosperity,
> That so live here as ye should never hence,
> Remember death and look here upon me.
> Ensample I think there may no better be.
> Your self wot well that in this realm was I
> Your queen but late, and lo now here I lie.
>
> Was I not born of old worthy lineage?
> Was not my mother queen, my father king?
> Was I not a kingës fere in marriage?
> Had I not plenty of every pleasant thing?
> Merciful God, this is a strange reckoning:
> Richesse, honour, wealth, and ancestry
> Hath me forsaken and lo now here I lie.
>
> If worship might have kept me, I had not gone.
> If wit might have me saved, I needed not fear.
> If money might have holp, I lackèd none.
> But O good God, what vaileth all this gear?
> When death is come, thy mighty messenger,
> Obey we must, there is no remedy,
> Me hath he summoned, and lo now here I lie.
>
> Yet was I late promisèd otherwise,
> This year to live in wealth and delice.

Lo whereto cometh thy blandishing promise,
O false astrology and divinatrice,
Of Goddës secrets making thy self so wise.
How true is for this year thy prophecy!
The year yet lasteth, and lo now here I lie.

O brittle wealth, ay full of bitterness,
Thy single pleasure doubled is with pain.
Account my sorrow first and my distress,
In sundry wise, and reckon there again,
The joy that I have had, and I dare sayn,
For all my honour, endured yet have I
More woe than wealth, and lo now here I lie.

Where are our castles, now where are our towers,
Goodly Richmond, soon art thou gone from me;
At Westminster that costly work of yours,
Mine own dear Lord, now shall I never see.
Almighty God, vouchsafe to grant that ye
For you and your children well may edify.
My palace builded is, and lo now here I lie.

Adieu mine own dear spouse, my worthy lord,
The faithful love that did us both combine
In marriage and peaceable concord,
Into your handës here I clean resign,
To be bestowed upon your children and mine;
Erst were you father, and now must ye supply
The mother's part also, for lo now here I lie.

Farewell my daughter, Lady Margarete.
God wot full oft it grieved hath my mind,
That ye should go where we should seldom meet.
Now am I gone, and have left you behind.
O mortal folk, that we be very blind.
That we least fear, full oft it is most nigh;
From you depart I first, and lo now here I lie.

Farewell Madam, my lord's worthy mother,
Comfort your son, and be ye of good cheer,
Take all a worth, for it will be no other.
Farewell, my daughter, Katherine, late the fere
To prince Arthur mine own child so dear,
It booteth not for me to weep or cry,
Pray for my soul, for lo now here I lie.

Adieu Lord Henry, my loving son adieu.
Our lord increase your honour and estate.
Adieu my daughter Mary, bright of hue,
God make you virtuous wise and fortunate.
Adieu sweet heart, my little daughter Kate,
Thou shalt, sweet babe, such is thy destiny,
Thy mother never know, for lo now here I lie.

Lady Cicely, Anne, and Katherine,
Farewell, my well beloved sisters three.
O lady Bridget other sister mine,
Lo, here the end of worldly vanity.
Now well are ye that earthly folly flee,
And heavenly thingës love and magnify,
Farewell and pray for me, for lo now here I lie.

Adieu my lords, adieu my ladies all,
Adieu my faithful servants every one,
Adieu my commons whom I never shall
See in this world, wherefore to thee alone,
Immortal God verily three and one,
I me commend—thy infinite mercy,
Shew to thy servant, for lo now here I lie."

But if, except for More and Skelton, there were no poets, there were those who produced books—printed, copied, written. The King's Privy Purse accounts are full of " rewards " to them; as ten pounds to a Frenchman "for printed books"; as much to Richard Pynson who "opened a press for mass-books to be printed" in 1505—he had been a law printer till then, and in the year of the King's death he introduced Roman type into England; various sums to Quintyn Paulet the librarian for the King's books and their bindings; the heavy sum of £46, 10s. "to Henry Jacob for certain books delivered to the friars at Richmond by a letter signed." There is even one entry: "for a reward given at the paper-mill, 16s. 8d."

It is true there are as many entries on odd offerings or amusements—many payments for the King's losses at cards and tennis; payments for lions, gerfalcons, eagles, leopards; to the fools; to the abbot of misrule; for the morris dance; payments for the costs of keeping the Pretender, including his tailor, £2; payments to gardeners and actors and trumpeters and astronomers and dancers and tumblers, for certain priests who impeached men, and constables and others who hunted men down, for "a glistening stone" and a musk-ball, for garnishing armour and spices for hippocras, for bonfires; to a "stranger of Purpynyan (? Perpignan) that showed quintessentia"; "to Oliver Tonor for relics"; for the burial of the Earl of Warwick; "to a fellow for eating of coals"; "to a stranger of Constantinople"; "to my lord of York, to play at dice "; " to the great woman of Flanders "; " for my Lord Prince's pardon (*i.e.* indulgence) "; for the King's confessor's new coat, and to the smith at Richmond for a little clock; for one that made a list of divers Kings; for tabernacles of gold and mass books; for images; to the Scottish boy with the beard.

But beside these court items of policy, piety, or play, there are others of a different kind. Remote as Henry made himself, and dangerous as he was to all tall crops, he seems to have been willing to be familiar with the low. He followed the policy, if not (like the Black Prince) the doctrine, of largesse. But it is pleasant, and possible, to believe it was more than that; that the King preferred perhaps the entries of gifts to this peasant or that woman before his entries of payments to spies and to those who brought evidence. Beer drunk at a farmer's house; " one that was hurt with a gun "; the maidens of Lambeth for a May; a man of Southwark wrongfully arrested; two reapers in two fields; one that had corn trodden down; a woman that was with child; John Smethe of Barnstaple that was wrongfully peached and brought up; a woman that gave the King cherries and strawberries, and another that gave the King posies; one that was hurt with a chariot; a poor man that sueth for his house; the wives of Canterbury for their light; a woman for two glasses of water

(5s. ; the New Testament was correct when it promised a reward) ; a Welshman for making a rhyme ; a man for a present of peascods ; the boys at Bath ; a priest that wrestled ; a little maiden that danced (£12—an incredible sum !) ; one that blew on a horn ; the heretic at Canterbury (whom, according to Bacon, the King "though no schoolman," converted by argument ; anyhow, the heretic got 6s. 8d.) ; the binding of the Keeper's daughter of Westminster to prenticehood ; redeeming of persons out of the King's Bench ; a woman for a red rose (1499 ; the White being in custody at Westminster may have given Henry extra pleasure in the red) ; the harvest folk beside Burnham Abbey ; a poor man that had his corn eaten by the King's deer. . . .

And so on. Remote as it all is, it is yet a kind of distant Tudor note. Henry was sounding it in those harvest fields and to those women who brought fruit and flowers. It is a note sounding between policy and preference, the note that Elizabeth afterwards felt in her heart, the note that enjoyed the common people. We can hardly say that Henry enjoyed the people—or anything. His son enjoyed women and theology ; and one granddaughter took joy in adoration and heavenly love and the other world, and one in culture and cerebral passion and this, but of the joy of the founder of their House there is no sign.

This is perhaps the great lack; it is this which leaves the eyes void and leaves only a face of wax, or if ever a human, then a human face watching without gladness and listening without peace.

Only, besides music and hunting, there is one thing of which we know—architecture. He built a palace at Sheen; after it had been burnt down he built another on the site, and called it Richmond. He caused work to be done on St. George's Chapel at Windsor, St. George being the patron saint chosen for the heir of England, Prince Arthur. But the greatest of works with which Henry was architecturally connected—after the Tudor monarchy—was the Lady Chapel at Westminster. The King, said Bishop Fisher, had a singular and special devotion to the Blessed Virgin. In his will he caused to be written:

"I trust that by the special grace and mercy of thy most Blessed Mother Ever Virgin, Our Lady Saint Mary, to whom, after thee, in this mortal life hath ever been my most singular trust and confidence, to whom in all my necessities I have made my continual refuge, and by whom I have hitherto in all mine adversities ever had my special comfort and relief, will now in my most extreme need, of her infinite pity take my soul into her hands, and it present unto her most Dear Son: Wherefore, Sweetest Lady of Mercy, Very Mother and Virgin, Well of Pity, and Surest Refuge of all needful, most humbly, most entirely and most heartily I beseech thee;

and for my comfort in this behalf I trust also to the singular mediations and prayers of all the holy company of heaven ; that is to say, Angels, Archangels, Patriarchs, Prophets, Apostles, Evangelists, Martyrs, Confessors, and Virgins, and specially to mine accustomed Avoures (Patrons and Advocates) I call and cry, Saint Michael, Saint John Baptist, Saint John Evangelist, Saint George, Saint Anthony, Saint Edward, Saint Vincent, Saint Anne, Saint Mary Magdalen, and Saint Barbara ; humbly beseeching you, not only at the hour of death so to aid, succour and defend me, that the ancient and ghostly enemy nor none other evil or damnable spirit have no power to invade me nor with his terribleness to annoy me, but also with your holy prayers to be intercessors and mediators unto our Maker and Redeemer for the remission of my sins and salvation of my soul."

One would like to know the name of the architect of those sentences as we know the name of the architect of the chapel. It was Robert Vertue ; and William Bolton, Prior of St. Bartholomew's, Smithfield, was the Master of the Works.

" It is far in advance of anything of contemporary date in England, or France, or Italy, or Spain. It shews us Gothic architecture not sinking into senile decay, as some have idly taught, but bursting forth, Phœnix-like, into new life, instinct with the freshness, originality, and inventiveness of youth ; searching out paths which none had adventured before, subjecting the ancient problems to a new analysis, and solving them in a fashion equally surprising and delightful. This Royal chapel in deed

THE KING IN HIS STATE 177

and truth is, as Leland well styled it, an 'Orbis Miraculum.'

"The vault, to begin with, is the most wonderful work of masonry ever put together by the hand of man." [1]

And again :

"Gothic construction was on the verge of a totally new and startling development ; retaining vaults, it was able to dispense with the machinery of buttress, flying buttress, and pinnacle. So far from " carrying within it the inherent elements of its own dissolution " Gothic architecture was on the point of running a new race even more marvellous than that of old. Vertue had taught how to build vaulted fanes on pillars ; others, retaining walls, might have had façades as uniform and symmetrical as those of any palace of the Renaissance, unbroken by obstructive buttress or fretful pinnacle. Such was the golden prospect which opened forth to English Gothic in the first years of the sixteenth century, of which this Royal chapel was the harbinger." [2]

It was begun in 1502, when Warbeck and Warwick were dead. If he did not design, Henry at least approved the plans. By the time of the King's death in 1509 the fabric was finished up to the vault. It was to be the burial place of Henry VI, translated from Windsor and, if the Pope would consent, canonized ; also of Elizabeth of York ; also of the King himself. There was

[1] Francis Bond, *Westminster Abbey*, Part V. chap. xv. Oxford University Press.
[2] *Ibid.*

to be a perpetual endowment of something like £100,000 ; to provide for three chantry priests, two lay brothers, three scholars, and thirteen almsmen, with three poor women to wait on them. The endowment was to cover masses and devotions, with almsgiving, in twenty-one other churches. The King's will arranged for ten thousand masses. He intended to keep (though perhaps he did not see it so) as magnificent a state for his corpse and his soul as ever he kept before they separated. He created wonders ; he multiplied devotions, being (as Bacon might have said) a little poor in that multiplication. He overmuch admired wealth ; ten thousand masses are only bearable when they are a reckless gesture. They could not be that in him ; they have, therefore, a little of the rhetoric of superstition in their mere number.

It is to be hoped he had the masses ; probably he did, for his son Henry VIII had "a singular and special devotion" to the Blessed Sacrament. It is almost all the father had. Certainly he was buried in his chapel of Our Lady, but Henry VI was left at Windsor, and all the inner planning of his chapel was spoilt. "Henry VII dies, and Henry VIII upsets the whole plan at once and ruins the chapel for ever." The son also took over the endowment, and the appointments of the chapel. The body of Katherine of Valois, who had married Owen

THE KING IN HIS STATE 179

Tudor and mothered the line, had been wrapped in lead and laid aside till the Chapel was built. It was left to lie. Two hundred and fifty years afterward Pepys saw her lying there; the lead had been broken away. " I did have the upper part of her body in my hands, and I did kiss her mouth." It was the last of her kisses; after being interred in 1776, she was finally buried in 1878 by Dean Stanley under the altar of the Annunciation in the Chapel of Henry V.

Such was the far and faint end of the King's intentions; such the end of the great new architectural movement. But indeed that last is only a sign of a greater thing even than itself. There was a whole movement of passion rushing up at that time; the vault of Christendom was to be re-principled; the energy of religion was to initiate its art anew. In the year 1490 Greek began to be taught at Oxford; in the year 1499 Erasmus, then round about thirty, first came to England, and met John Colet at Oxford. " One biographer after another," says Professor R. W. Chambers, " has felt that it was this friendship with Colet which definitely decided the bent of Erasmus's many-sided mind."

One cannot envy the great creative minds; one can hardly envy Erasmus; but one may a little envy Colet—to have influenced Erasmus! It was on this visit that he wrote the famous letter in praise of English studies. " I have met with so much kindness and so much learning, not hackneyed and trivial, but deep, exact, ancient, Latin and Greek, that I am not hankering so much after Italy. . . . It is marvellous how widespread and how abundant is the harvest of ancient learning which is flourishing in this country. All the more reason for your returning to it quickly. From London, in haste." The letter was written on 5th December 1499. It was a Thursday, exactly a week after the execution of Warwick. The King who had executed Warwick had no passion, or no opportunity, for the joy of learning. His youth had hardly given him the chance. But, like a self-made captain of industry, he was determined that his son should have the education and the friends he had never had. Even Morton, even Fox, were rather great administrators than great scholars; they were men of this world, even if good men, and not of the world of sanctity or of the world of the imagination to which scholarship belongs. It is true that Morton at any rate represents another side of the new energy, but it is its traditional side, it is the passion for Reform. There has never been an age when the Church has not clamoured that the Church should reform the Church; no, not the Apostolic; no, not our own. Purity throbs in Christendom like its pulse; it is the sign of its life. Morton desired purity in the Church and also among the clergy, which is not at all the same thing. But Morton died next year, in 1500, and as if with his death Reform flagged. Scholarship surged on alone, producing its own eccentricities by the help of the printed page, and it was, on the whole, an unreformed authority that tried to deal with those eccentricities. The personification of that flagging of reform is the figure of that man whom also the King set on his way—Thomas Wolsey. Wolsey in 1499 was senior bursar at Oxford and a fellow of Magdalen ; unintroduced, so far as we know, to the King and Prince Henry.

Prince Henry was a boy of eight, and was already taking his pleasure in the new intellectual excitements, though not yet the competent, if uninspired, theologian he was to become. Erasmus was staying with the Lord Mountjoy near Greenwich. Thomas More took him and another friend for a walk as far as Eltham. He carried them into the great hall of the palace ; there was an array of the household, there were the royal children, Henry and the rest, except Arthur. " In the midst stood Henry . . . with a certain royal demeanour ; I mean a dignity of mind, combined with a remarkable courtesy." More saluted the Prince, offered him some tribute of written composition, presented Erasmus. They remained to dinner. The Prince, of his own accord or on suggestion, sent Erasmus a note " inviting something from my pen." Erasmus, a little annoyed at being caught wanting, went home and wrote a poem in praise of Henry VII and all that was his. When, however, he left England, he found himself in disagreement with the King on what was his. Henry had forbidden the carrying of gold or silver coin out of the kingdom. Erasmus (advised, he said, by More) thought that the decree might not, for reasons, apply to the £20 he was carrying. He was wrong; the King's officers seized most of it, and Erasmus never quite forgave the English.

The two episodes present the King in his whole relation to the New Learning. He encouraged it when and as he could and cared to; he engaged it around the Throne and the children of the Throne. Scholarship, however, had to pay as well as any other occupation. But the real moral of the Eltham meeting is not only in the often-stressed, ironical friendship and fate of Henry and More. It is the figure of the eight-year-old boy, given every chance by his devoted father, and afterwards spoiling and twisting all his father had begun to do—harming the dynasty, spending the money, ruining the alliances, and discountenancing the high and glorious invention of new art which the architects had planned in the Lady Chapel at Westminster.

And beyond England—to the West?

Nothing very much. The King left it to others to discover new continents—whether actual or philosophical. He paid a little; he fitted out a ship or two; he encouraged. Ships had been going out before he took an interest; Bristol had sent out expeditions in search of " the island of Brazil and the seven cities." Bartholomew Columbus, searching for help for his brother, came to England to ask for it, but he did not find any. In 1495 John Cabot came to the King. By now Henry was more settled, and he knew what Columbus had done. He conceived that Cabot might do as much for him. He gave him permission to go with five ships and take possession of any territory he found on behalf of the King of England. A fifth of all profit was to go to the King. Eventually Henry went so far as to take over a fifth of the cost and fit out one of the five ships. They returned in 1497 with news of discovered land. The King had found a possible makeweight for the Spanish empire, and he was willing to spend more on making it actual. The Spanish ambassadors protested; Henry became unsympathetic. That interview was to be the first of many; already even Henry was unconsciously formulating the maxim of so much war and massacre : " no peace with Spain beyond the line." A hundred years afterwards the great-grandson of Henry, James I, was to throw his hat to the ground and shout with anger at the Spanish ambassador protesting against the wrongs committed by Raleigh. It is true James gave way in the end to the demands of the ambassador, but then James loved justice and peace. Henry neither shouted nor gave way. He proceeded to fit out at his own expense another five ships and send them out in 1498.

But apparently no discoveries were made. The King took no more interest, except to issue a permission or so to various persons to go, find out, and lay hold on anything they could. He desired rather to consolidate than to explore and increase. He gave £20 to those merchants who had been in the " new found land "; it was enough.

CHAPTER VIII

THE HUNTING OF SUFFOLK

THE first part of Henry's reign had been troubled by Simnel and Perkin, Pretenders who were, one way or another, serious threats to himself and his desired dynasty. The trouble, in those years, was definite and exterior. In the later years there is a renewed trouble, but it is rather an interior thing, a haunting of the mind. The King could not forget his danger. In 1506 he was still pursuing it; away in Croatia, on their way to the King of Hungary at Buda, two English ambassadors were riding to demand the surrender of the man then designated by that recurring phrase—" the White Rose." It is the contemporary phrase used by the diplomats—" the White Rose of England, the enemy of the King of England." But the last two Roses were thornless, it seems, everywhere but in Henry's dreams. It was he who pursued them, not they who dared him, yet the pursuit was as careful and persistent as all the King's work.

The sister of Richard III had married John de la Pole, Duke of Suffolk. He was neither of the Blood himself nor had he any hostility to the

Tudor. He had accepted Bosworth; he stood by Henry at his coronation, carrying the sceptre, and he stood by him afterwards. His sons, however, on the mother's side were Plantagenet, and Richard, after his own son died, had named the elder, the Earl of Lincoln, as his successor. At first the Earl of Lincoln went with his father. He accepted Bosworth; he followed Henry against the Lovel rebellion of 1486. In the next year, however, after taking part in the Council held at Sheen against Simnel, he had fled—first to the Dowager Duchess of Burgundy in Flanders, and then to Ireland, in order to support Simnel. He was killed at Stoke, and his lands were seized by the Crown, after attainder.

This was in 1487. In 1491 the father, the Duke of Suffolk, also died. The title and lands would have devolved on the next son, Edmund, if the King had not intervened. Accepting the opportunity to pursue his policy of reducing the power and position of the Families, Henry refused to recognize the ducal rank of Edmund, on the ground that the income and dignity had been so much diminished by the attainder that Edmund was incapable of maintaining a proper ducal magnificence. He consented to allow Edmund to re-purchase a part of the lands by cash payments, made by instalments, but he insisted that the dignity must not be higher than an Earldom. It was consequently the Earl of Suffolk who, in 1494, took part in the ceremonies and glories which accompanied the installation of Prince Henry as Duke of York, and on the second day achieved one of the prizes. It was the Earl who in 1495 received the King at his own house of Ewelme. Yet he was known as the Duke; in 1497 the Venetian ambassador wrote that he had been introduced to the King by the Bishop of London and the Duke of Suffolk. Certainly there lingered in his own mind the thought of his high, his almost royal—perhaps, if everything were kept in mind, his quite royal—rank. He was a man " stout and bold of courage, and of wit rash and heady." It was his disadvantage and his ruin.

In 1499 he killed " a mean person." That was not his ruin. It might have happened to any member of the Families, and the King was ready to pardon him. But before he could be pardoned, he must be tried. Neither he nor any of rank were to be any more exempt from the King's peace. That was the meaning of the oath which had been sworn in the King's first Parliament, and the firm intention of the King's policy since. Suffolk was indicted in the Court of King's Bench. He was very angry. The tradition of aristocracy, the past of his family, goaded him. He saw himself as forced into the common Courts by a man who was occupying a seat which should have been his dead brother's, and depreciating a nobility greater, even infinitely because of that lost royalty, than his own. Henry Tudor had robbed him of the Throne, of the duchy, and now even of decency; the thing was " a great maim and blemish to his honour." He determined to leave England, and secretly he crossed to Guisnes, to its governor, James Tyrrel, there to nurse his displeasure.

It was the year of Warbeck's landing. Henry could not afford to have so grand a discontent abroad, and he was willing to appease it if possible. Guisnes was a great deal too near Flanders and the Duchess to please him. He caused inquiries to be made and the ports to be watched; otherwise, he waved olives. One of his innumerable embassies—on its way to the Archduke Philip in Flanders—was commissioned to persuade Suffolk to return. Sir Richard Guildford, the King's controller, was its head. The King provided it with a careful and complex set of instructions. He foresaw that Suffolk might refuse to return unless in the company of the ambassadors as a safeguard. He was, if possible, to be dissuaded from this, and to be encouraged to bring Sir James Tyrrel with him instead. If, however, Suffolk thought Sir James hardly good enough, and insisted, then the ambassadors might abandon their journey and content the Earl by returning with him. It was more important to the King at that time to placate Suffolk than the Archduke.

It was most important that, at a moment when he was succeeding in his foreign policy, and when one Pretender had only recently been driven from the palaces of Europe, another all-but Pretender should not enter them.

But if Suffolk refused to return ? Then Sir Richard was to point out, privately, " as it were without the King's knowledge," that all the continental sovereigns, or at least France, Spain, Portugal, Naples, Scotland, the Archduke, Milan, were bound by treaties not to " receive, favour, succour, entertain, or suffer him in any manner of wise to abide or remain in any place or places of their obeisances, but to his utter clear destruction, take and send him to the king." So, Sir Richard was to ask him (" sadly "), what would he do ? Also, in order to impress him, a formal public summons was to be made to him at Calais to return.

But if still he did not return ? if he were determined to go on ? Sir Richard was to point out that, this obstinacy and disobedience notwithstanding, if Suffolk did nothing too outrageous, the King might still show favour to him in the future. He was to hesitate before he did anything that would make it impossible for Henry to overlook it ; that is, before he behaved anywhere in any manner but as the King's true and faithful subject, faithful even if fretful ; that is, before he breathed a syllable against the right of the still somewhat uneasy head that wore the crown.

Henry had again provided, as far as he could, for all eventualities; the phrase "but if not" doubles through these instructions as through all. Suffolk might even be shown them or something like them; might be given them to take and study them at leisure in his own lodgings. He was to be given every opportunity; the serpent dispatched the dove into the Earl's bosom—if only he would harbour it. Anything to keep another Claimant from renewing disturbance. The Earl meditated and agreed. He returned. He was immediately taken into favour. He accompanied the King in 1500 on a journey to Calais. It is about this time that Sir Robert Curzon enters the story.

Curzon, like Clifford, is one of those persons for whose behaviour there can always be found a reason, and yet the reason is never quite sufficient for the behaviour. He had ridden beside Suffolk in Prince Henry's tourney in 22nd June 1491. In 1499, when Suffolk fled from England, he was Governor of Hammes Castle. Soon after Suffolk's return Curzon asked the King for leave to go and fight against the Turks, and obtained it. Henry always had a kind of lingering tenderness for the idea of a Crusade; it was the kind of pious act which he could understand. Curzon was told to what officers he must surrender

Hammes. He obeyed; he set out for the East; on his way he went through Flanders. It seems probable that at the King's instructions he made secret inquiries there upon many Yorkist intrigues into which Suffolk had entered; it is to be remembered that Warwick was still in the Tower. From there he disappeared into the Christian wars.

He reappeared presently, at the court of Maximilian, with a reputation. Maximilian made him a Baron of the Empire, and they talked of politics. The hostility which the King of the Romans felt for the King of England had not been lessened by the compulsory political alliance of the two or by the execution of the man whom Maximilian still regarded as Duke of York. The conversation dealt with the Tudor's "murders and tyrannies." Maximilian heard of the de la Poles and their claim; he recklessly declared himself willing and eager to support their claim. Curzon let Suffolk know of this tenderness. Suffolk, who had not up to then had any experience of Maximilian, showed himself still more willing and eager to take advantage of it. In the summer of 1501, a couple of months before the arrival of Katherine, he left England for the second time. In France apparently he met Curzon and then went on to the Tyrol, to put himself under the protection and beg for the support of Maximilian. "This sad chance," wrote the chronicler, "I think happened among the great joys and solaces of King Henry lest that he might not by overmuch forget himself."

It was not a thing Henry was likely to do, and indeed he had now passed the point when he could. Vigil was becoming an obsession with him; his policy was becoming his master. When he knew that Suffolk was with Maximilian, he caused the Earl, Curzon, and others, to be proclaimed traitors. That was natural enough; it was natural, though less decent, that he should strike at relatives and acquaintances. Suffolk's brother, Lord William de la Pole, and his cousin, Lord William Courtenay, were arrested and imprisoned. On the other hand, another brother, Richard de la Pole, was left untouched; the reason given is that he was "an expert and politic man who so craftily conveyed and wisely ordered himself in this stormy tempest, that he was not entrapped either with net or snare."

The proclamation was made on 7th November, less than a week before the marriage of Arthur and Katherine. It is impossible, reading the phrase "he was not entrapped either with net or snare," not to recall that other phrase: "The King arranged with some of Perkin's attendants that they should suggest to Perkin . . ." Such phrases are not to be trusted as historical evidence, but they show of what Henry was believed capable at the time. He was thought to have the intention, the care, and the subtlety, to destroy not only the Pretender whom he had in captivity, but also the whole house of the De la Poles. The Princess of Wales must be married to an undoubted heir. It cannot, of course, be supposed at the same time that Henry was trying to drive Suffolk abroad and that he objected to Suffolk being abroad. But the operations of his spies and agents may have produced an effect beyond his immediate wishes, and the fall of the family left a migratory thorn of the White Rose to prick him.

Another personage was also caught by nets and snares. If Suffolk's account can be at all trusted, Sir James Tyrrel, who had returned to his post at Guisnes, was seized by treachery. He was persuaded to surrender himself to a safe-conduct ; he was then compelled, by a threat of immediate death, to order his son to surrender the castle ; he and his son were then brought back to the Tower. There he is said to have confessed to the murder of the Princes in the Tower. At least such a confession finally prevented any future claimant to their identities. Tyrrel, having confessed, was executed in May 1502. By then the señor Prince Arthur was himself dead, and on the tenth of the same month Ferdinand and Isabella were sending secret commissions by a new ambassador to conclude another marriage—between Katherine and the young Prince Henry. It was no wonder that the Princess thought of her first nuptials as consecrated in blood; she might have said it of her second also.

Maximilian, however, was not so happy to find Suffolk at his door expecting help as Henry was irritated to know him there. The King of the Romans would have been only too willing to oust Henry, but he had very much to do and very little to do it with. Besides which the presence of Suffolk was now definitely displeasing to the Sovereigns of Spain, who sent messages begging that the fugitive should be delivered back to the King of England; at least, let him not be allowed to remain in the imperial dominions. Henry was talking of a loan to Maximilian for the Turkish wars, and any loan seemed a good thing. The conversations with Suffolk remained vaguely hopeful. They dealt with men and money; three thousand and five thousand soldiers were mentioned. Suffolk had believed Maximilian's promises to be definite and binding; he had arrived in expectation of support. He eventually found himself marooned at Aix-la-Chapelle. Behind him, out of England, the persistent energy of the King of England was seeking to recapture him.

The death of Prince Arthur raised his hopes. There were only two lives between the Throne and his chance of the Throne. The worst reports

THE HUNTING OF SUFFOLK

of Henry's own health were abroad; he "was not able to live long." "Say," wrote Suffolk to his agent, "when you speak to the Sacred Majesty of my affairs: 'If Henry's second son were dead, there would be no doubt of my lord's title.'" In fact, when King Henry was ill in 1503 and discussions opened among the lords, it was remarked that "none spake of my lord prince," but some of Buckingham and some of De la Pole. The lieutenants of the castles of Guisnes and Calais determined to retreat into their castles, hold aloof, and make peace with whoever became master. But neither did. Suffolk's letter was dated 12th May 1502. On 19th June, Henry's ambassadors signed a treaty with the King of the Romans. By this, ten thousand pounds was to be paid over for use against the Turks, "which sum he of long time hath desired of your Grace." The money was subject to a pair of Henry's alternatives. If Maximilian would consent to expel from the Imperial dominions all rebels against the English King, "though they should be Dukes," the money was to be a gift; if not, it was to be a loan. Maximilian accepted the first alternative, the more willingly since he later discovered that Aix was a Free City, and he could not compel Suffolk to leave. He made gestures; he ceased to send Suffolk any money to live on, and he promised the burgomaster of Aix to pay the Earl's debts

more or less on condition that he left the city.
The Earl inquired of astrologers what were the
favourable hours for his taking a " privy journey,"
and the King of England continually made efforts
" to engage some of the servants of E. de la Pole
always to give intelligence."

The King was willing to abandon £10,000 in
order to recover Suffolk. When he found he had
paid this to no immediate end he looked round
for other means. The Hansard merchants had
through the reign formed one of those groups
which, along with the Families, the rich, and the
Plantagenets, he had tried to depress. He had
set himself, in Miss Temperley's words, " to vindicate the position of his own subjects, and to restrain the privileges of the Hansards." He continually made efforts to break their monopolies
of trade. The only occasion on which his policy
was favourable to them was in 1493 when his
interference with the Flanders trade caused the
Steelyard riot—and that was because of Warbeck
—and in 1504. But where in 1493 he was dealing
with a real danger, in 1504 it was a shadow that
drove him. Suffolk at Aix was helpless and harmless enough, but the King would not be content
to leave him there. His very attention to that
single beggared exile set up strange ideas. " The
King of England fears him greatly," it was said
in 1503. Driven by this shadowy fear, the King
made approaches to the Hansard confederation.

THE HUNTING OF SUFFOLK

He abandoned the restrictions he had tried to impose; he restored their privileges. There was a possibility that through their influence he might yet get his hands on the fugitive. But before this vein could be worked, in April 1504, Suffolk left Aix, and the King abandoned the Hanse. In July 1504, Sir Robert Curzon had returned and been granted a pardon. The Earl, hoping nothing further from Maximilian, wrote to the Duke of Guelders, asking permission to cross the Duchy in order to reach Saxony. The Duke granted the safe-conduct, and broke it. Suffolk was seized and held in custody. The difference between his position and that of Warbeck in old days is clear. It had once been a question of who should have Warbeck to use against Henry; now it was a question of who could make profit by handing Suffolk over to Henry. It is true the difference is due to Henry's diplomacy, but it is true that by now he was in some danger of wrecking his diplomacy in his eagerness to gain that single point. No one of the Princes really believed in Suffolk's possibilities. James of Scotland wrote to the Duke:

"One of two things I think you are attempting —either that the King of England through vain fear shall conciliate De la Pole, or that he shall expect to see him restored by your arms. It is nonsense talking of fear in a king hitherto unconquered, whose friendship the greatest princes eagerly embrace, and who by his bravery has repeatedly overcome, with great slaughter, strong bands of enemies ; and as to restoring De la Pole in England, if you or the greatest prince of all Europe entertained such a notion, and if De la Pole had conspired to bring in a rebel, the enterprise might lead to greater difficulties, and be remembered for ages. Beware. This Edmund will deceive you by too much promising of friends ; he, who lately, after actually returning, and being fully restored to his friends by the King, fled from his country and supporters in poverty and dearth of friends. I wish, therefore, you had refrained from empty threats, and talking of his boasted power."

Presently the Earl became even less important. The Duke of Guelders submitted to the Archduke (who was now, owing to the death of Isabella, the King of Castile), and the Earl was handed over and handed back as chance dictated. He was kept in close guard. His brother Richard, who had followed him from England and was still at Aix, wrote pathetically to him :

SIRE,
I recommend myself humbly to your grace. Please it you to know that the burgesses of Aix have returned from the king of Castile. What answer they have had from him I know not, but within four days after their return came to me Martin host of the Pot, and divers others, meeting me in the street, and demanding their

money of me. I gave them the best answer I could to
satisfy them. At last they said to me, " Your brother
is the falsest man that ever was of his promise, and we
will do to him as he ought to be served. We will accuse
him in this town and all the other towns belonging to
the empire, that all the world may know that he is a
false perjured man ; and we will have our money from
you. And if you will not find a remedy for us, we will
find one for ourselves ; and therefore make your answer
to us in all haste."

Sire, as far as I can perceive they have some encouragement to do this, putting your grace to such dishonour, and me also to dishonour and great personal
danger ; for I am apprised by two persons who are my
good friends, that king H. has desired the burgesses of
Aix to deliver me three leagues out of the town of Aix,
and he will pay them. And so I am advised no longer
to go into the street, for if I am killed in the street,
king Henry will pay them their money. I think in very
truth, it was done to the end that I might be the more
willing to do king Henry's pleasure, which is to abandon
you and do as he shall command me ; which would be
to your dishonour and mine all our lives long. Nevertheless, sire, if you will do towards me as I have
deserved, and as a brother ought to do to his brother
who is here in hostage for you, and I see that you
do the best to ransom me according to your promise,
you will find me your loyal brother, come what
may.

Sire, I request you likewise, if the case be that the
burgesses accuse you in this town where I am, to your
great dishonour and mine, as they say they intend to do,
do your best to declare yourself an honourable man, as a
good and honourable man ought to do, as you would

find me your good and true brother, as you have done and always will do, in so doing. Please it you to give credence to Eustace, bearer of these. Sire, I have heard news of Derik. I have hope that he will bring us good news without fail. No more, except that God give you good and long life. Written at Aix, the 24th day of November 1505,
    by your loyal brother,
         RICHARD SUFFOLK.
To my lord my brother.

It was at this time and as the prison of his world grew closer that the Earl's sense of sovereignty increased. He sat in his prison at Namur and drew up Instructions for his Commissioners. He was preparing to submit, but, in a very madness of *hubris*, he would submit as an equal. He wrote as a prologue : " Be it known to all princes, nobles, and true Christian men, by this present writing, that we, Edmund duke of Suffolk, of England, on the 26th day of December last past had certain communications and words touching the troubles that are in the realm of England, by reason that it standeth betwixt the king of England and me as it doeth."

The articles followed. He wrote :

 1. He was willing to receive the King's pardon.
 2. He was to be acknowledged and fully installed as Duke of Suffolk, with restitution of all honours and lands as in the time of the Duke his father, with all such offices as his father or grandfather had held. And

of all monies spent out of the revenues from the time of his father's death.

3. Certain towns which had been alienated (even in the time of Edward IV) were to be restored, and whatever the Duke his father had done in such matters should be annulled. And all the money restored.

4. If the King of Castile should detain him, King Henry was to be besought to "help him to his liberty."

5. If he should die without male issue, his widow to have her jointure, and his daughter her inheritance.

6. The agreement to be drawn up in writing, sealed, and confirmed by the King, the Prince, and the Parliament.

7. All his friends to be freed, their goods and lands and honours restored; or any who have died in his cause, their heirs to have possession.

"At the castle of Namur, the 28th day of January, the year of Our Lord God, a thousand, Vc and six.— EDMUND SUFFOLK."

"At the castle of Namur"! The fantasy that had possessed him so long had established itself in his brain. While he ingeniously devised terms the King, his enemy, was devising a treaty that ended his terms. Providence had intervened once more, as so often, and now so unnecessarily, on behalf of the Tudor. A storm had prevented him reaching England in time for Buckingham's rebellion, a storm had overthrown Buckingham and left Henry to make himself King, a storm had almost prevented the arrival of the Spanish girl who was to be fatal to the monarchy he had established, a storm now threw his last enemy into his hands.

Philip, son of Maximilian and so Archduke of Austria, son-in-law of Isabella of Castile, and now (by her death) King of Castile, with his wife Juana, had set out by sea from Flanders for Spain. Among others in their train was the ambassador to Philip from the Signory of Venice. His account of the voyage is as follows:

" King Philip and Queen Juana embarked at Armuyden on the 7th instant with their whole retinue, but, in order to await the full moon, the fleet did not go out of port until the morning of the 10th. The wind was then fair, and continued so the whole of that day and the next until off Hampton, when towards midnight, after a dead calm, every ship having all sail set, so violent a storm sprang up from the N.N.E., as greatly to alarm the oldest and most experienced hands, for the night was dark and the channel unsafe, and great was the labour and peril of lowering the sails. That night one-third of the fleet parted company; and the wind lasted the whole of the 12th, taking them to the edge of the Bay of Biscay, so far as the pilots could ascertain from their soundings. A calm then ensued, and continued until the evening of the 13th, when the wind rose from the W.S.W., full upon the coast of England. Orders were then given to tack throughout the night, in the hopes of a change for the better, but the sea and wind rose so highly, that about midnight, when possibly not more than 50 miles from the shore, and when such was the darkness that not an object could be distinguished one span ahead, a terrible hurricane commenced, of which the oldest mariners in the fleet say they have not experienced the like within the last half-century. All now sought for safety as they best might: some ships stood out to sea, others made for land; amongst the latter was his [the ambassador's] ship. At daybreak eighteen sail found themselves in a dense haze so close upon the land that all gave themselves up for lost."

He attributed their safe arrival in Falmouth to the miraculous mercy of the Almighty. Meanwhile, the King and Queen had taken the other tack and remained out at sea in the gale the whole of the 14th and 15th, when, with only two ships, they were driven into Portland. Of their adventures the Ambassador wrote :

"Whilst waiting for a messenger to convey the accompanying letter to the consul in London, a gentleman arrived at Falmouth sent by King Philip to notify his well being and his determination to come towards Falmouth by land.

"Never had man a narrower escape from drowning than the King. His ship was at sea all Wednesday and until Thursday evening, unable to make any port; the guns and everything else on deck were thrown overboard. When attempting to lower the mainsail, a gust of wind laid it on the sea, carrying the ship gunwale under; nor did she right for half an hour. Had it not been for the aid given by one single mariner, who thrice plunged into the waves and, by cutting away the shrouds, righted the vessel, their plight would have been irremediable; for both the master, the pilots, and the crew were utterly bewildered, and had given themselves up for lost. In the meanwhile the vessel caught fire thrice, so that the chance of death in the flames or in the deep was equal. For a long while the King bore up manfully, always in his doublet about the ship, encouraging everybody; but at length a sea struck him, and he was hurled below with such violence that everybody thought he was killed. Thenceforth he remained with the Queen, who evinced intrepidity throughout; and the King and some of his gentlemen to whom he is affectionately attached, having embraced each other mutually, awaited immediate death, without any hope of escape. The King declared that he did not regret his own death, since such was the will of God; but deeply lamented, first of all, that he should cause the death of so many brave men whom he had brought with him, as he firmly believed that since his own ship, which was the biggest, and manned by so many pilots and skilful mariners, perished, there could be no salvation for the rest of the fleet. Secondly, he grieved to leave his children orphans at so tender an age; and thirdly, he deplored the ruin and confusion that might ensue in his territories."

He was, however, saved. News went to London, and on 31st January, King Henry in great state received his royal and shipwrecked guests at Windsor. There followed months of grand ceremonies and secret talk. Henry was by this time plotting against Ferdinand, but that can be conveniently discussed presently. Among the great affairs of Princes at freedom, Henry never took his eyes from the small affairs of the pseudo-Duke in prison. Bacon heard or invented an account of the affair which is probably unjustified, but is still Bacon.

"But while these things were in handling, the King choosing a fit time, and drawing the King of Castile into a room where they two only were private, and laying his hand civilly upon his arm, and changing his countenance a little from a countenance of entertainment, said to him, Sir, you have been saved upon my coast, I hope you will not suffer me to wreck upon yours. The King of Castile asked him what he meant by that speech? I mean it (saith the King) by that same harebrain fellow my subject the Earl of Suffolk, who is protected in your country, and begins to play the fool, when all others are weary of it. The King of Castile answered, I had thought, Sir, your felicity had been above those thoughts. But if it trouble you, I will banish him. The King replied, those hornets were best in their nest, and worst when they did fly abroad; and that his desire was to have him delivered to him. The King of Castile herewith a little confused, and in a study, said, That can I not do with my honour, and less with yours; for you will be thought to have used me as a prisoner. The King presently said, Then the matter is at an end. For I will take that dishonour upon me, and so your honour is saved. The King of Castile, who had the King in great estimation, and besides remembered where he was, and knew not what use he might have of the King's amity; for that himself was new in his state of Spain, and unsettled both with his father-in-law and with his people; composing his countenance, said, Sir, you give law to me; but so will I to you. You shall have him, but upon your honour you shall not take his life. The King embracing him said, Agreed. Saith the King of Castile, Neither shall it dislike you, if I send to him in such a fashion as he may partly come with his own goodwill. The King said it was well thought of; and if it pleased him he would join with him in sending to the Earl a message to that purpose."

It was arranged. A gentleman of King Philip's crossed to Flanders to bring back the Earl. No one knows what he said to him. The custodians were reluctant to surrender him till it was certain the King of Castile had left England. Shipwrecked royalties were held sometimes to hard terms; as Harold Godwinson had been, on a near coast, four hundred and fifty years before. It was feared the King of England might, after obtaining the White Rose, have power to demand some other greater concession. Philip had to send more letters by another messenger. On 16th March 1506, Edmund de la Pole was brought to Calais by a small escort; on 24th March, he landed at Dover. He was immediately fetched to London and to the Tower. His life had been promised and was left him, for seven years. After—it is to be hoped—dreaming great dreams of making equal contracts with the captor who had sought him so long, he went out to death under the eighth Henry in 1513.

There remains, two years later, and less than a year before the seventh Henry's death, one other picture of the King concerned with such a matter. It was 19th June 1508, and the King rode in his garden on a horse; beside him on a mule the Provost of Cassel. They were talking diplomacy; then presently the King turned to another matter. "He told me," wrote the Provost to his mistress, the Duchess of Savoy, "how, six or seven days ago, he had ordered the lords of his council to speak to me of some of his rebel subjects and others who daily do him blame and dishonour of whom a list was given me which I send you.

"Madame," the Provost continued, "I do not know how to tell you how much he has this thing at heart . . . those contained in the said list sent prisoners that right may be done on them . . . those who are his subjects, and for the others that the like justice should be done there, without pretence or any warning by which they may save themselves.

"Madame, I never knew he had the thing so much at heart. God knows how shamed I was by him, and what things he said to me. Certainly I would rather be elsewhere than to be mixed again with such a thing. He took nothing well of all that I could say.

"Madame, I am too heavy at heart to write what I heard. I make an end."

It is one of the very few pictures of Henry Tudor—riding there in his garden, over-topping the abashed and troubled Provost, and speaking in the June sunlight of his enemies, and that no warning should be given by which they could save themselves. The Provost was not able to say anything that was taken well.

They talked for three hours, and that was the end—" Madame, jay le ceur trop pesant a voz en escriere ce que jay ouy, par quay en iray fin." The King was plotting how to drive Ferdinand from Castile—the adventurer of Bosworth had come far enough—but the other matter was nearer his heart. A month later the Provost wrote a hasty note urging the despatch of ambassadors, and said in it : " Comme je voz ay escrit par tant de fois, le roy Dengleterre a toutjours espie le Fortue "—(" as I have written to you so often, the King of England has always been on the watch for Fortune ").

Richard de la Pole, Suffolk's brother, died at Pavia in 1425.

" The King said, Then the matter is at an end. For I will take that dishonour upon me, and so your honour is saved." It may (if indeed it were ever used) have been but a light phrase ; more likely it is Francis Bacon's own invention. It is paralleled by another later : " (Morton) was willing also to take envy from the King more than the King was willing to put on him. For the King cared not for subterfuges, but would stand envy, and appear in any thing that was to his mind." The implications are right. Henry Tudor was never afraid of what the world would call dishonour. He was never afraid of dishonour. He was not swayed by words or by the opinions of others; it is perhaps why he left few words and no opinions of his own. He had his strength. His point of honour was to have none, none at least that could be affected by the world about him. He belonged to his world, but he was never afraid of it; only it seems in the end he was a little afraid of God, as better men than he have been. Apart from that last fear (held off not only by the ten thousand masses of his will, but by as many ordered at divers Lents, and by prayers perpetually purchased), he was altogether free. No councillor, no officer, no spy, had any power on him at all. He could listen and look and look them down. He had no image of himself to maintain before them or even before himself. He kept silence, but he never kept pretence; it did not matter to him what anyone thought, only what they did. In that sense he was alone always; it is that solitude which surrounds him, even to us, with an alien quietude. His greatest biographer said elsewhere that solitude was only fitting to a god or a beast; he might have noted that it was in some sort also possible to Henry Tudor.

CHAPTER IX

THE NATURE OF THE KING

IN that prison of himself, the King pushed his actions every way towards their extreme. The last two or three years produce a kind of caricature of the comprehensible policy and person of the earlier. The alteration of temper, the exaggeration of habit, is marked by two deaths; perhaps it is attributable to two deaths. The Cardinal Morton, Archbishop and Chancellor, had died in 1500; he was eighty. The Prince Arthur had died in 1502; he was sixteen. The chief means and the chief purpose of Henry's activities changed in two years; he had to find substitutes, and the substitutes were the cause of a less prosperous future.

The Cardinal-Chancellor had been a person of marked capacity and strength. He had been—so long before—instrumental in procuring the recognition of Henry as leader of the discontented in England; he had been of much service to Henry in exile; he had been brought into the most intimate circle of the Court; he was recommended by Henry to the Pope for the Hat, and he remained intimate and faithful to the end.

He was believed by some, both on the Continent and at home, to have great influence with the King; others believed that the King was ruled by none and very little given to be influenced by any. The rebels in 1497 were reported to have demanded the surrender to them of Morton among others. On his death the City Chronicler wrote that he was "a man worthy of memory for his many great acts and specially for his great wisdom . . . in our time was no man like to be compared with him in all things; albeit that he lived not without the great disdain and great hatred of the Commons of this land."

Two greater men left us their judgment of Morton, Bacon and More: "He was a wise man," said Bacon, "and an eloquent . . . but in his nature harsh and haughty . . . envied by the nobility and hated of the people. . . . He won the King with secrecy and diligence, but chiefly because he was his old servant in his less fortunes and also for that in his affections he was not without an inveterate malice against the House of York. . . . In the matter of exactions, time did after show that the Bishop in feeding the King's humour did rather temper it. But whatsoever else was in the man, he deserveth a most happy memory, in that he was the principal means of joining the two Roses."

More modifies for us the harshness and haughtiness of which Bacon had heard. "He had great delight many times with rough speech to his suitors, to prove, but without harm, what prompt wit, and what bold spirit were in every man. In the which, as in a virtue much agreeing with his nature, so that therewith were not joined impudency, he took great delectation. And the same person, as apt and meet to have an administration in the weal public, he did lovingly embrace."

It seems that the reports of his roughness to suitors, and the reports of his intolerance to taxpayers, were both exaggerated. The famous dilemma which was called " Morton's Fork "— that the man who spent money must have it to spend, and could pay taxes ; and he who spent no money must have it in saving, and could pay taxes—arose from what Bacon described as his willingness " to take envy from the King more than the King was willing to put on him." But certainly he was one of the King's chief servants ; his influence, if it did not much affect the King concerning others, affected others concerning the King. He was one of those who built the Tudor throne, and he set the colour of the civil servants of the Tudors. He believed in a strong government and a single nation, and he lived before the religious controversy began. What action he would have taken had he been in Cranmer's place thirty-three years later is not to be guessed. But the relation of this Cardinal-

THE NATURE OF THE KING 213

Chancellor of Canterbury with the Throne and the more and more exalted figure upon the Throne, followed by the relation of his successor Wolsey the Cardinal-Chancellor of York with the Throne and the exalted Prince, went far to determine the attitude of Cranmer and his clergy; especially because, in those years, the Cardinal-Chancellors were often dealing with the Roman pontiff in his aspect as an Italian prince of inconvenient political demands.

He died, and after him others of the older men, such as Sir Reginald Bray, who was also blamed for the taxes, and, according to Bacon, "had with the King the greatest freedom of any councillor, but it was a freedom the better to set off flattery." He was said also to take the freedom sometimes "humbly to reprehend the King." Of Richard Fox, who outlived his master, it was said that his face showed "authority and goodness." All that group, neither controlling nor directing, would and did expostulate and protest; they had about them something of a public morality, and they modified that morality, if at all, only in the extreme need of the State. There was in them all a remainder of honour; they tried to remind the King of his honour. He did not need them less because he was not concerned with honour. Few did as much for the King's son.

They died; and Arthur died, and (to quote

Bacon once more) "nature, which many times is happily contained and refrained by some bonds of fortune, began to take place in the King." He adds: "Carrying on with a strong tide his affections and thoughts unto the gathering and heaping up of treasure." But, as was said before, Francis Bacon had always a strong dislike to heaping up treasures; he loosed his money as magnificently as his mind, and spent his having in all ways at once. It was not merely treasure of gold that was Henry's preoccupation, though that was part of it; it was his whole nature which, released from the restraint of fortune, hurried along its own channels. On the national side the death of Morton left lesser men free to profit by the King; on the foreign, the death of Arthur made him think it necessary to find new profit for himself. Nor, as he grew older, did he forget the profit of religion: he built his chapel; he thought of a crusade.

The successors of Morton were Empson and Dudley—the history of the first ends with himself, but the tale of the second runs on through the Tudor line: his son, the Duke of Northumberland, almost collected the Crown for the family; one grandson, Lord Guildford, died for treason to Mary; another, Lord Robert, was the lover of Elizabeth. His family, that is to say, remained of account for all the resentment felt against their founder. It was not forgotten that

THE NATURE OF THE KING

they, however unwisely, had served the Throne. It is true that both Edmund Dudley and Sir Richard Empson were executed by Henry VIII in the year after his father's death. But that was partly brought about by their rash behaviour in arming their servants during the King's last illness. The young King was willing enough to recover the reputation of the dynasty and to achieve a reputation for himself by decapitating two gentlemen who had seemed to arm against himself.

It was a poor return for their service to his father. As Henry VII's reign went by and the King found the actual danger of revolt or riot less, he did not lose his habit of vigilance. The high lords of battle had been cut down; the farthest lineal claimants to royal rank were in Hungary or enclosed in the Tower. He did not propose to allow a new power of nobility to establish itself instead of the old. His care attacked anyone who seemed likely to be overnoticeable except as the King's servant, and the City suffered for its riches. The King would no more allow financial magnates to grow up than aristocratic. Capitalism was changing; financial capitalism was the new method of economic civilization. But the King was determined that it should be capitalism tempered by exactions, as the earlier method had been capitalism tempered by executions. The laws of England were at his command, and the spies who discovered new treasons were matched by the extortioners who discovered new illegalities. It was tyrannical, but the King had every intention of being a tyrant; it was his aim. He took some pride in doing it legally, for the laws were part of his personal hobby. Ancient laws were refurbished; new laws were created. " Whoever raised himself above what was, in Henry's opinion, his proper sphere was at once energetically suppressed."[1] It is not at times a very pleasing picture. But neither have we found the success of the capitalists, after the King's effort was defeated in the days of his successors, a very pleasing picture.

An instance was the proceeding against Sir William Capell. He was the son of a Suffolk gentleman, and he became a rich draper of Walbrook, and Alderman of his Ward. His first difficulty was in 1495, the year when the French King was raiding Italy and Warbeck riding off the South Coast and when, to save a small thing among the great, "a bawd of the Stews side" named Togood stood in the pillory at Cornhill on 2nd July, for fetching two women from Queenhithe, " and intended to have had the said women to the Stews there to have done him service as common women." (Thus the white slave traffic as well as capitalism appears in all centuries.) The King's policy had ruled that all

[1] *England under the Tudors*, W. Busch. 1895.

THE NATURE OF THE KING

purchases by foreigners should be paid for at once in money or goods, just as it ruled that foreigners must not take gold out of the country. Sir William was " condemned to the King " for breaking the statutes, and made his peace by heavy payments. In 1504 he became Lord Mayor. In 1508 the royal ministers attacked him again " for things done by him in the time of his mayoralty " ; it was alleged that he had been lax in his duty, especially in not properly punishing a coiner. The accusation was certainly intended to produce a composition such as Capell had consented to pay in 1495. But this time the ex-Lord Mayor was obstinate in his riches. He was first imprisoned in the Counter, and afterwards when his matter had been brought before the Council was taken to the Tower. The fine put on him was two thousand pounds, which he refused to pay, declaring in a symbolical phrase that recurs through English history that " the King had no authority in the City of London." He remained in the Tower till Henry's death, when he was released and immediately again chosen Lord Mayor. The agent in the whole affair was Dudley.

A more famous victim, but that not so much for money as for revenge, was the father of Thomas More. In 1504 the young Thomas—he was twenty-six—was sitting in the House of Commons. Professor R. W. Chambers does not know his constituency, nor therefore does anyone. It was the year in which Henry had determined to make a little money out of Parliament, for the marriage of the Princess Margaret to the King of Scotland. He asked for £90,000 ; he got £40,000, and he did not raise all that. Among the speakers was More, who argued against the grant. One of the King's household, a certain Master Tyler, reported More's action to him. Henry did not allow the outrage on his will to pass, but he would not strike directly at More ; he did not suppose that the young man was rich enough to pay anything, and the King was never one to waste energy. The biographer of More reports that he "devised a causeless quarrel" with the elder More, and had him thrown into the Tower. There he stayed until he consented to pay a hundred pounds, under some colour of legality. It was, like so much else in the reign, the precursor of a more dreadful quarrel in the time of the two young sons.

In fact the later years of Henry's policy saw him undertaking a series of raids against the rich. "The possession of wealth was punished as if it were a crime. They, Empson and Dudley, drew over England a net which few men of position or substance escaped."[1] The methods were indefensible. But at least there was another side. The City Chronicle says of the year 1506-7:

[1] *Henry VII*. Gladys Temperley. Constable. 1914.

THE NATURE OF THE KING

" And this year was a wonderful easy and soft winter, without storms or frost. And this year the King of his goodness delivered out of all prisons in London as many prisoners as lay for forty shillings and under. And this year was Thomas Kneysworth, late mayor, and his two sheriffs condemned to the King in great sums of money, after painful prisonment by them in the Marshalsea sustained."

The royal Robin Hood lacked the manners and mode of his more famous predecessor of Sherwood. No one quite trusted him. The release of the prisoners was due probably to the King's method of piety; the persecution of the rich to his policy. But that Christian doctrine which Henry hardly ever seems to have grasped insists that we must be fair even to the rich, and it seems that Empson and Dudley were not. Bacon was not one to twist law on either side, and Bacon disapproved.

" For first their manner was to cause divers subjects to be indicted of sundry crimes; and so far forth to proceed in form of law; but when the bills were found, then presently to commit them; and, nevertheless, not to produce them in any reasonable time to their answer; but to suffer them to languish long in prison, and by sundry artificial devices and terrors to extort from them great fines and ransoms, which they termed compositions and mitigations.

" Neither did they, towards the end, observe so much as the half-face of justice, in proceeding by indictment;

but sent forth their precepts to attach men and convent them before themselves and some others at their private houses, in a court of commission ; and there used to shuffle up a summary proceeding by examination, without trial of jury ; assuming to themselves there to deal both in pleas of the crown and controversies civil.

" Then did they also use to inthral and charge the subjects' lands with tenures *in capite*, by finding false offices, and thereby to work upon them for wardships, liveries, premier seisins, and alienations (being the fruits of those tenures) ; refusing (upon divers pretexts and delays) to admit men to traverse those false offices, according to the law.

" Nay, the King's wards after they had accomplished their full age could not be suffered to have livery of their lands without paying excessive fines, far exceeding all reasonable rates.

" They did also vex men with information on intrusion, upon scarce colourable titles.

" When men were outlawed in personal actions, they would not permit them to purchase their charters of pardon, except they paid great and intolerable sums ; standing upon the strict point of law, which upon outlawries giveth forfeiture of goods. Nay, contrary to all law and colour, they maintained the King ought to have the half of men's lands and rents, during the space of full two years, for a pain in case of outlawry. They would also ruffle with jurors and inforce them to find as they would direct, and (if they did not) convent them, imprison them, and fine them.

" These and many other courses, fitter to be buried than repeated, they had of preying upon the people ; both like tame hawks for their master, and like wild hawks for themselves ; insomuch as they grew to great

THE NATURE OF THE KING 221

riches and substance. But their principal working was upon penal laws, wherein they spared none great or small; nor considered whether the law were possible or impossible, in use or obsolete; but raked over all old and new statutes; though many of them were made with intention rather of terror than of rigour; ever having a rabble of promoters, questmongers, and leading jurors at their command; so as they could have any thing found, either for fact or valuation."

This is perhaps the best place to quote also the famous story of Henry and the Earl of Oxford:

"There remaineth to this day a report, that the King was on a time entertained by the Earl of Oxford (that was his principal servant both for war and peace) nobly and sumptuously, at his castle at Henningham. And at the King's going away, the Earl's servants stood in a seemly manner in their livery coats with cognizances ranged on both sides, and made the King a lane. The King called the Earl to him, and said, My lord, I have heard much of your hospitality, but I see it is greater than the speech. These handsome gentlemen and yeomen which I see on both sides of me are (sure) your menial servants. The Earl smiled and said, It may please your Grace, that were not for mine ease. They are most of them my retainers, that are comen to do me service at such a time as this, and chiefly to see your Grace. The King started a little, and said, By my faith (my lord) I thank you for my good cheer, but I may not endure to have any laws broken in my sight. My attorney must speak with you. And it is part of the report, that the Earl compounded for no less than fifteen thousand marks. And to show further the King's extreme diligence; I do remember to have seen long since a book of accompt of Empson's, that has the King's hand almost to every leaf by way of signing, and was in some places postilled in the margent with the King's hand likewise, where was this rememrance.

"Item, received, of such a one, five marks, for a pardon to be procured; and if the pardon do not pass, the money to be repaid; except the party be some other ways satisfied.

"And over against, this memorandum—'otherwise satisfied' (of the King's own hand), which I do the rather mention because it shows in the King a nearness, but yet with a kind of justness. So these little sands and grains of gold and silver (as it seemeth) help not a little to make up the great heap and bank."

Stebbing, from whose text the quotation is taken, adds:

"A heavier fine for a similar offence was exacted from Lord Abergavenny some years afterwards. In a memorandum of obligations and sums of money received by Edmund Dudley for fines and duties to be paid to the King . . . the following item appears as belonging to the twenty-third year of the reign:

"' Item: delivered three exemplifications under the seal of the L. of King's Bench of the confession and condemnation of the Lord Burgavenny for such retainers as he was indicted of in Kent; which amounteth unto for his part only after the rate of the months 69,900 *l.* '

"It appears from the Calendar of Patent Rolls

(23 Hen. VII, Part II. p. 18) that George Nevile, Knt., Lord Burgavenny received a pardon of all felonies, offences against the forest laws, etc., on the 18th of February 1507-8 : two months before Henry's death. Fabyan mentions his being committed to the Tower ' for a certain displeasure which concerned no treason ' in May 1506."

While the pursuit of the rich went on at home, the search for brides went on abroad. It was heartily encouraged. Arthur had died on 2nd April 1502. On 15th April Ferdinand and Isabella were writing to De Puebla saying that they were glad to hear he and Katherine were in good health. Nor had the news reached them by 29th April when they were again writing to explain how they were urging Maximilian to hand Suffolk over to Henry, and to discuss what should be done with the money collected in England for use against the Turks ; they were clear it should not go to the Pope, " for should the Pope get it into his hands it would be employed for other purposes." But before 10th May they had heard of Arthur's death and had taken action. They prepared at Toledo three documents—two commissions and a letter. The commissions were made out to Ferdinand, Duke de Estrada, an officer of the household, " a mediocre man " as the Princess Katherine called him. One has three clauses ; Estrada was to require the repayment of the hundred thousand scudos which had been paid as the first instalment of the marriage dowry, to demand that all " towns, manors, and lands " promised to her on marriage (which were to amount to " one-third of the revenues of Wales, Cornwall, and Chester ") should be immediately handed over, and to arrange for the return of the Princess to Spain in the shortest time possible.

This was the official demand. But if Ferdinand put forward as his claim the return of the Princess conveying the money paid by Spain and promised by England, it was no less the intention of the King of England to retain the Princess with the money paid and the money promised. Actually both Kings had their eyes fixed on another possible bridegroom—the younger brother of Arthur, Henry, Duke of York. The second commission to Estrada of the same date empowered him to conclude a treaty of marriage between Katherine and Henry, and to settle the terms. The letter was to De Puebla, and commanded him to obey the Duke de Estrada in all things, " as if he were Ourselves." Two days later the sovereigns dispatched another letter in which they had time to think of grief. The death of Arthur, they said, had renewed all their past afflictions, but God's will must be obeyed.

Letters followed one another swiftly through May and June. Henry was in the strongest position because he was in control of all the three items in dispute—the Princess, the hundred thousand scudos, and the lands, etc. He also had De Puebla more or less in his pocket. It was already feared that he would do nothing except ask for the rest of the dowry, and possibly offer the young Henry as a substitute for Arthur. The Spanish sovereigns still yearned for some political action against France. They set to work to make it clear that all the expenses of their daughter's household must fall on Henry. They forbade her to dispose of any of her gold or jewels. She was to be given her lands and manors and sent home. Estrada was to urge her return. " Do this in such a way that he may believe we are desirous of it." It was felt that Henry must want to do something about this liability.

He displayed no anxiety for the new marriage. Each side was anxious for the other to make proposals first. He seems to have let it be supposed that he hoped, by giving the Princess her revenues, to be free to retain the scudos. The Spanish sovereigns, on the other hand, said that this would be an outrage. On 16th June they wrote to Estrada, mentioning for the first time the matter that was to be of such importance in a few years—the consummation of the marriage. Up to now it had not occurred to them. Estrada was to get at the truth ; he must be as persuasive and flattering as he could in order to find out. On 12th July Isabella herself wrote. Sinister news of movements of troops and of possible proposals of marriages for Prince Henry had come from France. Estrada was to hurry everything up; delay was dangerous; the mistress of Katherine's household had written that the marriage had certainly not been consummated; hurry, hurry. But show no sign of hurry; be prudent, be cool. And talk to the King of England about the possible recovery of Guienne and Normandy. The Spanish sovereigns put infinite faith in the effect of this mirage.

Through July and August the letters continued, all to the same effect. Estrada was to bluff Henry into the marriage, by demanding the Spanish scudos or by promising the French provinces. He was to play the departure of Katherine for all it was worth. " Speak of her loss and affliction," wrote Isabella, " speak of her need for consolation and her age; say that we cannot endure that a daughter whom we love should be so far from us in her grief. The one purpose of this business is to bring the betrothal (with Henry) to a conclusion . . . for then we shall be able to seek the help of England against France." De Puebla was to be used to talk to the King about Normandy and Guienne. The unfortunate De Puebla was by now being pushed about by both sides. It was through him that the wildest proposals were to be made to Henry; it was probably through him that Henry was making it clear that he had no intention of returning the scudos nor much belief in the gain of the provinces. It was enough for him to pay the thousand pounds to the King of the Romans in order to secure the exclusion of Suffolk from the Empire. He was rather expected to explain that law was on his side and that money paid as part of a marriage portion was not paid back; at least the Spanish sovereigns had written declaring that both civil and common law compelled it, and if Henry's own did not, yet " we are not subject to the laws of his kingdom." It would be, they said, inhuman of him; the Princess must be returned —but " the one purpose of this is to bring the betrothal to a conclusion."

By September the betrothal had been at least mentioned, and some draft treaty sketched. Henry let the discussions drag. It was not he who wanted to go to war anywhere or to use the arms of Spain. The young Henry had been created Prince of Wales in May 1502, and he was no small matrimonial plum. But in the next year he was suddenly thrown back into the second place from which, so far as marriage proposals were concerned, he had emerged for awhile. For on 1st February 1503 the Queen gave birth to a girl child in the Tower; on 11th February she died. King Henry himself suddenly became eligible for any European princess who might be thought suitable.

His first thought was Katherine herself. De

Puebla wrote to Isabella mentioning it as a thing " spoken of in England," which (De Puebla being regarded everywhere as Henry's confidant) probably meant by Henry or with Henry's presumed sanction. His letters had reached Isabella by 11th April, and considering the time letters took (on the precedent of Arthur's death) the proposal must have been made before the middle of March, a month or so after the Queen's death. Isabella was really shocked. She wrote to Estrada a letter in which something of anger at the proposal and something of irritation at the delay mingles with a hope of the betrothal and a consideration of policy :

" We have received letters in which we are informed of the death of the Queen of England, our sister. These tidings have, of a truth, caused us much grief, as we have declared more at length by our other letter, and in which we have spoken of the audience you are to seek, and the consolation you are to administer, on our part, to the King of England, our brother. Do as we have directed you in the said letter. The Doctor has also written to us concerning the marriage of the King of England with the Princess of Wales, our daughter, saying that it is spoken of in England. But as this would be a very evil thing, one never before seen, and the mere mention of which offends the ears—we would not for anything in the world that it should take place. Therefore, if anything be said to you about it, speak of it as a thing not to be endured. You must likewise say very decidedly that on no account would we allow it, or even hear it mentioned, in order that by these means the King of England may lose all hope of bringing it to pass, if he have any. For the conclusion of the betrothal of the Princess, our daughter, with the Prince of Wales, his son, would be rendered impossible if he were to nourish any such idea. . . .

"After you have had an audience of the King of England, and offered him a consolation on our part, you must set about bringing to a conclusion the betrothal of the Princess of Wales, our daughter, and the Prince of Wales. For it certainly seems a very grievous and strange thing to us that, after having conducted ourselves in this business with so much love and frankness towards the King of England, and with such pure heart and such a good will to preserve and increase the bonds of relationship and amity between ourselves, him, and our successors, he should desire to conclude the negotiation in the manner he does, especially when we consider his former wishes in regard to it. For, what he now requires, is neither that which in reason ought to be between such Princes, nor will our honour, nor that of the Princess of Wales, our daughter, permit that he should make use of such crooked expedients in these negotiations. Most certainly if there had been in our kingdoms a like Princess, the daughter of the King of England, who had come hither in the way that the Princess, our daughter, has gone to England, and if we had had to treat respecting her betrothal with our son, we would have guarded the honour of his daughter more jealously than even if she had been our own. And with much love and a right good-will would we have done all that in such a case would have had to be done, without making such turnings and twistings in the business. . . ."

The King of England can hardly be said to have made many more " turnings and twistings " in the business than Ferdinand and Isabella themselves, except in the last proposal. But now he reluctantly consented to allow something definite to happen. Even he could not indefinitely keep the royal widow without taking any steps, especially if Isabella were losing patience. He appointed a commission in June, and they and Estrada drew up a Treaty. The first clause pledged the Parties to apply, with all their influence, for a dispensation ; the second promised a contract of marriage within two months after the dispensation had been granted ; the third and fourth arranged for the payment of another hundred thousand scudos, and for the solemnization of the marriage as soon as Prince Henry was fourteen. The Treaty was ratified in Spain, and the sovereigns wrote a covering letter saying that Henry possessed " all and every virtue of a great king." They urged him again to take action against France, and they even wrote to Katherine, permitting and urging her to pledge her credit to raise two thousand men for war. What she might not do for her own comfort she was directed to do for the policy of her parents.

The dispensation was applied for in August. But that supreme traditional figure of the Renascence, Alexander VI, died before he consented, and Pius III, who succeeded, died before he consented. In December Julius II ascended the Papal Throne. It was expected by both Henry and Ferdinand that the dispensation would be granted at once. In fact even by the next July it had not come. Julius was then writing in the friendliest way to Henry to say that he had delayed in order to consider the case more maturely. He hinted that there were obstacles. It may be that the Pope had in mind Ferdinand's particular request that the dispensation should cover the possibility of the marriage having been consummated. It would be more prudent, the King of Spain had written, "as the English are much disposed to cavil." As late as 28th November Henry was protesting to Rome at the delay. A Bull was sent secretly to Spain in November 1504, and Ferdinand immediately dispatched a copy to Henry. The Pope was startled to hear of this; he said he had sent it only to console Isabella on her death-bed. But by the next March it officially reached England.

The Prince Henry was then thirteen. The dispensation had been first applied for sixteen months before when he was just twelve. It must have been clear even to his boyhood that the See of Rome had taken a very long time to decide to grant it. This would not so much have mattered if the Prince had had no greater interest in theology than his father. He had the same kind of piety, except that his own personal devotion was (all his life) rather to the Blessed Sacrament than to the Blessed Virgin. But the younger Henry had been given every opportunity of profiting by the Revival of Learning, and he had a small but sincere capacity for metaphysics, that is, for the theology of his day. There was in his mind, between him and Katherine, already a faint consciousness of the reluctance that emanated from the Roman See. It was increased in 1505 by an act of positive reluctance imposed on him by his father. For reasons, the King was willing to have an instrument on the other side. He caused the Prince, then fourteen, to execute it. It ran as follows (the translation is from Lord Herbert of Cherbury's *Life of Henry VIII* [1706]) :

" In the name of God, *Amen*. In the presence of you the Reverend Father in Christ, by the grace of God, and favour of the Apostolical See, *Richard*, Lord Bishop of *Winchester*; I, *Henry*, Prince of *Wales*, Duke of *Cornwall*, and Earl of *Chester*, do say, allege, and by this writing set forth ; that although in my Minority and Being not as yet arriv'd to ripeness of Age for giving my Consent, I have *de facto* contracted a Marriage with the most serene Lady *Catherine*, Daughter of the King of *Spain*, which Contract, although it be of it self invalid, imperfect, and of no effect and force, by reason of my said Minority ; yet because this Contract when I shall come to age and years of Consent, may appear and seem valid, and confirmed by tacit Consent, mutual Cohabitation, giving and receiving Tokens and Gifts,

THE NATURE OF THE KING 233

or any other determinate way ; for these Causes, I the foresaid *Henry*, Prince of *Wales*, now nearly arriv'd to maturity of Age, and being just at years of consent, do hereby Protest, that by any thing said or to be said, done, or to be done, I do not intend to ratify, confirm, or make valid the said pretended Contract of Marriage ; but by these Presents, being thereunto mov'd neither by force, craft, nor intreaty, but voluntarily, freely, and without any compulsion whatever, I do renounce and disclaim the said Contract ; and do resolve and intend by the most powerful means, in the most significant terms, and most effectual manner I can to renounce, disclaim, and dissent from the said pretended Marriage Contract, as the same is hereby renounc'd, disclaim'd, and dissented from. And I farther protest, that by any Word, Deed, Action, or Behaviour, said or done by my self, or by any other in my Name, or to be said, acted, done or perform'd by any person at any time, or in any manner whatsoever, I do not consent to the said Marriage Contract, or receive the said Lady *Catherine* as my lawful Spouse and Wife ; to all which Premises, this my Testimony is given, set forth and publish'd by me.— Henry, *Prince* of Wales.

" The above written Protestation was made and read by the most serene Prince the Lord *Henry*, before the Reverend Father in Christ, *Richard*, Lord Bishop of *Winchester*, who then sat Judge, and before me the under- written Notary Publick, who took it in Writing, in the presence of the under-written Witnesses, in the year of our Lord, 1505, in the eighth Indiction, in the second year of the Pontificate of our most Holy Father in Christ, by the Divine Providence, *Julius II*, Pope, on the 27th day of June, on which day his most serene Highness the

Prince, instantly order'd and demanded of me the said Notary, to draw up this publick Instrument, and the underwritten Witnesses thereto to bear Testimony. In proof and evidence of all which things, and every of them, his said most Serene Highness, the Prince, and the Witnesses, as is aforesaid, being thereunto call'd and requir'd, set their Names subscrib'd with their own Hands. The truth of all which I *John Read* testifie, by setting thereto my Hand and Seal Manual.—*G. Daubney, C. Somerset, Thomas Rowthale, Nicholas West, Henry Marny.*"

The result, so far as the King was concerned, was admirable. He had his son in a marriage which could be either a marriage or not as he chose. The Pope had allowed it, and it was therefore a marriage. But the bridegroom had formally refused his consent, and therefore it was no marriage. It was perhaps the greatest of the King's alternatives. He had it to hold in hand whenever he needed it. But it is not surprising if the youth who had experienced the Papal delay and had now sworn his own refusal were precisely the one person in England to be a little uncertain of the validity of the marriage. Upon that uncertainty, within a pious and superstitious mind, there supervened later on the undoubted fact that none of the six children of the marriage lived, except for one feeble girl. The protested nuptials produced dead child after dead child. It needed only Anne Boleyn to move him to violent action.

It was in 1504 that Estrada had written to Ferdinand : " It is not only from love that the King takes the Prince with him ; he wishes to improve him. Certainly there could be no better school in the world than the society of such a father as Henry VII. He is so wise and so attentive to everything ; nothing escapes his attention. There is no doubt the Prince has an excellent governor and steward in his father. If he lives ten years longer he will leave the Prince furnished with good habits, and with immense riches, and in as happy circumstances as man can be." The King did not live five. He left his son four things : a sense of the importance of the dynasty and therefore of an heir ; a sense of the need of killing all those who might be in the least dangerous ; a tendency to believe in signs and marvels ; and a sterile and doubtful marriage. That ceremony " in one of the lower chambers of the Palace of Richmond, in the eastern portion of it," had great results on English history. But the King thought no doubt that he was being very wise.

He had also, now, to be wise for himself. He was, in Stubbs' words, "the eligible parti of Europe ; the young pretender of fifty looking out for a wife." He did not forget a suggestion that Isabella had made and the Spaniards urged, a marriage with the Queen of Naples. De Puebla assured his sovereigns that the King and his

Council thought this marriage better than could be found elsewhere, " search all the world over. They lauded your Highnesses, on many accounts and for many considerations, above the Cherubim." But there was a condition :

" It seems a thing which ought not to be, and an improper thing, for the King to conclude such a marriage without being first certified by his ambassadors and envoys as to the person and appearance of the said Queen. For your Highnesses must know that if she were ugly, and not beautiful, the King of England would not have her for all the treasures in the world, nor would he dare to take her, the English thinking so much as they do about personal appearance."

In 1505, five days before the young Henry was making his declaration at Richmond, the English ambassadors had an audience of the proposed bride at Valencia. They had been charged with a questionnaire by the King on the appearance of the Queen of Naples, and they answered them. At first it seems a little repulsive that Henry, who has left us no intimate scandals of sex, who, if he loved his wife, which is doubtful, certainly loved no other woman, should inquire so closely into his bride's appearance and habits. It may be that there was something in him of that cerebral delight in sex which, overleaping a generation, appeared again in Elizabeth ; that he preferred, as she did, to contemplate it in his mind and did not care so

THE NATURE OF THE KING 237

much to enjoy it as objective fact. He had had to set a guard over himself all his life, and perhaps he could not, if he would, now abandon it; that also was to happen to his granddaughter, especially after the shock of the Seymour tragedy in her first adolescent love. But it is more likely that Henry did but do what he seemed to be doing—ask for information. He wanted to know.

The paper ran—in the relevant clauses—as follows :

"*Item, specially to mark and note well the age and stature of the said young queen, and the features of her body.*

" As to this article, as to the age of the said young queen, it is seven-and-twenty years and not much more ; and as to the stature of her person we cannot perfectly understand nor know, for commonly when that we came unto her presence her grace was sitting on a pillow, and other ij times we saw her going on her foot going overthwart a chamber that was not broad, where she came in at a door and came unto the queen her mother, being in the same chamber, and sat down by her, at the which both times she wore slippers after the manner of the country in such wise that we could not come to any perfect knowledge of the height of the said queen.

" And as to the features of her body of the said young queen, forasmuch as that at all times we have seen her grace ever she had a great mantle of cloth on her in such wise after the manner of that country that a man shall not lightly perceive anything except only the visage, wherefore we could not be in certain of any such features of her body, but as far as that we can perceive and judge that she is of no high stature but of a middle stature after our judgment by the reason of the height of her slippers whereof we have seen an ensample.

" *Item, specially to mark the favour of her visage, whether she be painted or not, and whether it be fat or lean, sharp or round, and whether her countenance be cheerful and amiable, frowning or melancholy, stedfast or light, or blushing in communication.*

" As to this article as far as that we can perceive or know, that the said queen is not painted, and the favour of her visage is after her stature, of a very good compass, and amiable, and somewhat round and fat, and the countenance cheerful, not frowning, and steadfast, and not light nor bold-hardy in speech, but with a demure womanly shamefaced countenance, and of few words, as that we could perceive as we can think that she uttered the fewer words by cause that the queen, her mother, was present, which had all the sayings, and the young queen sat as demure as a maiden, and some time talking with ladies that sat about her with a womanly laughing cheer and countenance, and with a good gravity, always the ladies talking with her having their countenances towards her grace with reverences and honour and obedience.

" *Item, to note the clearness of her skin.*

" As to this article, the said queen is very fair and clear of skin as far as that we could perceive by her visage, neck, and hands, the which we saw and well perceived.

" *Item, to note the colours of her hair.*

" As to this article, by that we could see and per-

THE NATURE OF THE KING

ceive and by the brows of the said queen, and by the ends of some of her hairs that we perceived through her kerchowes, it should seem her hair to be a brown hair of colour.

"*Item, to note well her eyes, brows, teeth, and lips.*

"As to this article, the eyes of the said queen be of colour brown, somewhat greyish; and her brows of a brown hair and very small, like a wire of hair; and her teeth fair and clean, and as far as we could perceive, well set; and her lips somewhat round and thick, according to the proportion of her visage, the which right well becometh the said queen.

"*Item, to mark well the fashion of her nose, and the height and breadth of her forehead.*

"As to this article, the fashion of her nose is a little rising in the midward, and a little coming or bowing towards the end, and she is much like nosed unto the queen her mother. And as to her forehead, the height or the breadth thereof we could not perfectly discern, for the manner of the wearing of the kerchowes or tucks in that country is such that a man cannot well judge it, for their kerchowes coming down to their brows, and much the less we could come by the very knowledge of that cause for that the queen weared black kerchowes.

"*Item, specially to note her complexion.*

"As to this article, as far as we can perceive the said queen is of a very fair sanguine complexion and clean.

"*Item, to mark her arms, whether they be great or small, long or short.*

"As to this article, as that we can perceive and know, that the arms of the said queen be somewhat round and not very small, by that we could perceive when that she putteth forth her hand when that we did kiss it ; and as to the length of her arm, to our understanding, it is of a good proportion according unto her personage and stature of height.

"*Item, to see her hands bare, and to note the fashion of them, whether the palm of her hand be thick or thin, and whether her hands be fat or lean, long or short.*"

" As to this article, we saw the hands of the said queen bare at three sundry times that we kissed her said hands, whereby we perceived the said queen to be right fair handed, and, according unto her personage they be somewhat fully and soft and fair and clean skinned.

"*Item, to note her fingers, whether they be long or short, small or great, broad, or narrow before.*"

" As to this article, the fingers of the said queen be right fair and small and of a meetly length and breadth before, according unto her personage very fair handed.

"*Item, to mark whether her neck be long or short, small or great.*"

" As to this article, the neck of the said queen is fully and comely, and not misshapen, nor very short nor long, but meetly after the proportion of her personage ; but her neck seemeth for to be the shorter because that her breasts be fully and somewhat big.

"*Item, to mark her breasts and paps, whether they be big or small.*"

" As to this article, the said queen's breasts be somewhat great and full ; and inasmuch as that they were trussed somewhat high, after the manner of the country, the which causeth her grace for to seem much the fullyer and her neck to be the shorter.

" *Item, to mark whether there appear any hair about her lips or not.*

" As to this article, as far as that we can perceive and see, the said queen hath no hair appearing about her lips nor mouth, but she is very clear skinned.

" *Item, that they endeavour them to speak with the said young queen fasting and that she may tell unto them some matter at length, and to approach as near to her mouth as they honestly may, to the intent that they may feel the condition of her breath, whether it be sweet or not, and to mark at every time when they speak with her if they feel any savour of spices, rosewater, or musk by the breath of her mouth or not.*

" To this article: we could never come unto the speech of the said queen fasting, wherefore we could nor might not attain to knowledge of that part of this article, notwithstanding at such other times as we have spoken and have had communication with the said queen, we have approached as nigh unto her visage as that conveniently we might do, and we could feel no savour of any spices or waters, and we think verily by the favour of her visage and cleanness of her complexion and of her mouth that the said queen is like for to be of a sweet savour and well eyred.

" *Item, to note the height of her stature, and to inquire whether she wear any slippers, and of what height her slippers be, to the intent they be not deceived in the very height and stature of her ; and if they may come to the height of her slippers, then to note the fashion of her foot.*

"As to this article of the height and stature of the said young queen, as in the vth article of this book it is answered that we could not come by the perfect knowledge of her height, forasmuch as that her grace weareth slippers after the manner of the country whereof we saw the fashion, the which be of vj fingers breadth, of height large, and her foot after the proportion of the same is but small, but by the slipper the greatness of her foot cannot be known, notwithstanding by the height of her slipper, considering the height that she appeared unto our sight being a-foot, her grace seemed not to be of high stature, and also by cause of the manner of the clothing that women do use and wear after the manner of the country, and also she of herself is somewhat round and well liking, the which causeth her grace for to seem lesser in height.

"*Item, to inquire of the manner of her diet, and whether she be a great feeder or drinker, and whether she useth often to eat or drink, and whether she drinketh wine or water or both.*

"As to this article, it hath been showed unto us by one Pastorell, the which is apothecary unto the said queen, and also by one Sorya, the which is a household servant, the which two persons be much in the presence of the said queen when that she eateth and drinketh, and as they do report and say, that the said queen is a good feeder, and eateth well her meat twice on a day, and that her grace drinketh not often, and that she drinketh most commonly water, and sometimes that water is boiled with cinnamon, and sometimes she drinketh ipocras, but not often."

The personal appearance of the Queen was not, however, to matter. Henry had a greater problem to solve, for on 26th November 1504 Isabella of Castile died, and European politics shifted. She had desired in her will that her husband, Ferdinand, should "administer" the kingdoms of Castile, Leon, and Granada on behalf of their daughter Juana. But their daughter Juana had been married to Maximilian's son the Archduke Philip. What would Philip say to this administration? And if there was a dispute, not to say war, who would be likely to win?

It affected profoundly all the diplomatic relationships. It also affected the daily life of the Princess Katherine. Up to March 1505 there were no letters of complaint from her. Henry had been showing a proper concern for her health, and she had even asked him to intervene in some difficulty among her servants, which like the young man in the Gospels he had formally refused to do, and had privately done. He had been properly paying her expenses. But by four months after the death of her mother, what with the delay in the dispensation, what with the decline in Ferdinand's prestige, what with the growth of the King's nature over his fortune, a change had taken place. There begin that series of letters from Katherine to her father which are at once pathetic and provocative. It is clear that Henry neglected the Princess — probably with deliberation. In 1505-6 she is writing that she is in debt for food, that she is all but naked, that the King of England will do nothing, though she has asked him with tears. As time went on, and Ferdinand paid no more of the agreed dowry, things became worse. Her servants (she said) were in rags, and she in destitution. The King of England was responsible for the agony of her life.

It is to be admitted that so were her own countrymen. It was perhaps natural that she should dislike and despise De Puebla. She continually warned her father against him. But the other ambassadors seemed no better to her. The Duke of Estrada was unsatisfactory. The last of all to arrive, the Knight Commander of Membrilla, whom at first she had wanted, became distasteful. There was trouble between the Princess's private household, especially her confessor, and all the embassies. She was in an unbearable position, and she was not a person to bear it. Yet she was compelled to bear it. Henry had no intention of letting her return to Spain; he had every intention of making her useful to him in England.

He kept her as an instrument. Her father had intended to use her in the same way, but he had lost control. He continually delayed to send the other payments of the marriage portion under the treaty, and his procrastination and Henry's exasperation ran level. De Puebla begged Ferdinand not to overvalue the jewels which were to be sent: "the King would resent it very much." Henry told Katherine that he did not regard either himself or his son as bound any longer to the marriage, as the money had not been paid. She asked De Puebla if this were legally possible; De Puebla said it was. She asked her confessor if it were morally permissible; her confessor said it was. She sent word to her father, who after a while wrote reassuring her. But through those years the marriage with Prince Henry was becoming her only hope. She was helpless to hasten it; she was not even allowed to see him. She felt that at any moment she might be dropped through a crack in the infinite negotiations, and left, alien and destitute, in England, without money, without husband. The marriage against which the young Henry had protested was the thing she needed most. So, indoctrinated by Fate and the Kings, the two young creatures came at last, after Henry was dead, to their nuptial-doom.

Meanwhile King Henry considered his possible brides. There was the Queen of Naples. But the King of the Romans had made another suggestion; he proposed his own daughter, the Archduchess Margaret. The King of France had suggested that Prince Henry might marry Margaret of Angoulême, a girl of thirteen. The King of England suggested himself as a bridegroom instead; the King of France raised no objection.

Alternatively, Henry discussed the possibility of marrying Margaret's mother, Louise. But the wildest possibility of all was to come.

It was in 1506 that Philip of Castile had been driven by storms to England, and besides the agreement for the delivery of the Earl of Suffolk, a marriage treaty was signed between them for the King's marriage with the Archduchess. But the Archduchess refused. She had been reported to be "very averse," but Maximilian went to see her in order to persuade her. He wrote to Henry to say so. Henry was not pleased; in his reply he referred to all the other grand offers that were being made him. Before any further serious efforts could be made to break down the obstinacy of the Archduchess, Philip had died in Spain, in September 1506.

As soon as Henry heard, he saw the possibility of a more profitable bride. Circumstances perhaps, rather than he, made the effort as insane as the bride. Juana's mind had been giving way for some time. It had been remarked while she was in England that she was becoming incapable of government, and if the Venetian ambassador remarked it, Henry can hardly have missed it. The King did not propose to let a weakness in his wife's mind hinder him from making her his wife. He had his eyes on Castile. The direct heir to Juana was her son Charles, but Ferdinand was known to be hostile to Charles. He would, he must have been as hostile to any prince, foreign or Spanish, who desired to establish himself in Castile; as much to Henry Tudor as to any. But this difficulty of diplomacy no more deterred Henry than the imbecility of Juana. He saw a royal widow, and he opened negotiations—as it were, automatically. The first instrument of the negotiations was the Princess Katherine.

She was the daughter of Ferdinand; she was the sister of Juana. She was directed to write to her father, proposing that her father-in-law (past and to come) should marry her sister; she obeyed. The King her father replied to her dubiously but cordially. "It is not yet known whether Queen Juana be inclined to marry again, but if she is it shall be with no other person than the King of England. . . . But the affair must be kept most secret, for if Juana should hear anything about it she would probably do something quite contrary."

Henry had been ill in the beginning of 1507, but he recovered, and during the year he pressed on with his proposals. He discussed with Maximilian his marriage with the Archduchess; with Ferdinand his marriage with the widowed Queen. He held the marriage of Prince Henry and Katherine in the background; he hurried on the negotiations of his daughter Mary with the Prince Charles of Castile. His involved policies complicated themselves with impossibilities. His daughter was to marry one claimant to Castile, and he was to marry another, and a third was to assist him. Yet he was at the same time hinting —in that afternoon ride through the garden— to the Provost of Cassel that he could help the King of the Romans to expel Ferdinand from Castile; he had (he said) a secret method which he would reveal to the King of the Romans alone. His alternatives had reached absurd heights; he let none slip; and he added to them a pious additional purpose—he began to agitate for a Crusade.

In past years, when it had been suggested, he had approved but demurred; he had said he would go when the Pope himself went. But as if his piety hastened in time with his policies, he now became anxious to begin. In 1505 the King of Portugal had taken up the idea and proposed it to Louis of France. Louis forwarded it to Henry. He said that if Henry were willing to go, he himself would. He rather desired to be associated with him " pour faire et accomplire le dit voiage et entreprise " than with any other king or prince of the world; and that if all other kings and princes failed, yet they three—the Lords of Portugal, France, and of England— would be strong and successful " en une si bonne et saincte querelle." One could not, the French king wrote, do anything of greater merit or more acceptable to our Creator.

THE NATURE OF THE KING

The great phrases seem to come from the mouths of an earlier age. The division of Western Christendom had not yet had its opportunity; all the mingled diplomacy and devotion of the West looked eastward to its enemy. In 1506 Henry Tudor was named by the Order of the Knights of Rhodes, "protector, champion, patron, and defender." It was perhaps one of the greatest tributes to his achievement—that the Order should have thought it worth while. In 1507 he wrote to the Pope, Julius II, urging an expedition against the Turks. Julius replied that his letters were "*gratæ et jocundæ*"; he would have them read in a Secret Consistory, both to Henry's glory and because they appertained "ad communem rem Christianam."

The tremendous phrase shatters the glory of the recipient. After such a youth and life, so careful, so industrious, so vigilant—to an oldish man mingling discussions of marriage with one reluctant bride and one imbecile—within a few months of that conversation in which the King insisted "that no warning should be given"; how do all those conditions fit with "the common Christian thing"? He was as Christian perhaps as most men in his realm or in Europe; in that sense he was common enough. But for anything worthy of the sublime phrase—the Pope was wrong. Henry did not know it, nor care to know it.

The King replied, in a letter throbbing with devotion, on 8th September 1507. He allowed that the Pope had difficulties ; kings were hard to be reconciled and crusades hard to initiate. But "for the common use and dignity of our Catholic Faith," and " the salvation of the souls of Christ's faithful," let it be firmly and surely resolved that no difficulty, no labour, should at all prevent the effort. Let the Crusade have more than one leader ; let a trinity of kings (" trinitas regum Occidente veniens ") seize with a strong hand the most holy Sepulchre of Christ from the hand of the infidels, and exhibit His presence corporally ("suamque præsentiam corporaliter exhiberet "). It is an odd sentence : how was Christ's presence to be corporally exhibited by the seizure and exposition of the Sepulchre ? Some clerk or cleric must have turned the phrase, which makes it more astonishing. Yet something of it hangs over all this, over the life and labour, over the crusades and the ten thousand masses, over the prayers and pomps of religion. They are there, and (no doubt) sincere. But they exhibit a sepulchre seized by the strong hand ; neither the illumination of the older world nor the enlightenment of the newer, neither Francis nor Erasmus.

Another, lesser, death had defeated Henry in another scheme. The Juana project had been applauded by everyone in the secret, in the "discreet manner of proceeding." De Puebla wrote that Henry would be the best husband in the world.

"As to the marriage of the Queen of Castile, the King of England and the few counsellors who are initiated in the matter approve fully of his discreet manner of proceeding. There is no king in the world who would make so good a husband to the Queen of Castile as the King of England, whether she be sane or insane."

He thought she would soon recover her reason when wedded to such a husband as Henry. King Ferdinand would at all events be sure to retain the regency of Castile. If the insanity of the Queen should prove incurable, it would perhaps not be inconvenient that she should live in England.

"The English seem little to mind her insanity, especially since he has assured them that her derangement of mind would not prevent her from bearing children."

Ferdinand answered that she should at least marry no other person than a King "so distinguished by his virtues." In September De Puebla was writing again that the King and his Council were longing for the marriage "even if worse things were said of the insanity," and on the same day Henry wrote to Katherine saying how well he was, and how shocked he was to hear she was in need of money. He sent her a little. The Princess took the view that "his words and professions had changed for the better" because of his eagerness for the marriage. "I should be afraid of him if the answer were not to accord with his wishes." In October the Princess herself wrote to her sister. She gave herself, certainly on Henry's instructions, to creating the fable of Henry's passionate love.

"Most noble and most mighty Princess, Queen and Lady, after having kissed the royal hands of your Highness and humbly commended myself to you, I have to express the very great pleasure it gave me to see you in this kingdom, and the distress which filled my heart, a few hours afterwards, on account of your sudden and hasty departure.

"My Lord the King was also much disappointed in consequence of it, and if he had acted as he secretly wished, he would, by every possible means, have prevented your journey. But, as he is a very passionate King, it was thought advisable by his Council that they should tell him he ought not to interfere between husband and wife. On which account, and for the sake of other mysterious causes with which I was very well acquainted, he concealed the feelings occasioned by the departure of your Highness, although it is very certain that it weighed much upon his heart.

"The great affection he has felt, and still feels, towards your Royal Highness from that time until now, is well known.

"If what my lord the King, our father, shall say to you should please, as I think it will please, your Highness, I do not doubt but that your Highness will become the most noble and the most powerful Queen in the world. Moreover, nothing will more conduce to your pleasure and satisfaction, and the security of the kingdom of your Highness. In addition to all this, it will double the affection subsisting between my lord the King, our father, and my lord, the King of England. It will also lead to the whole of Africa being conquered within a very short time, and in the hands of the Christian subjects of your Highness, and of my lord the King, our father. I entreat your Highness to pardon me for having written to you, and for having meddled in so great and high a matter. God knows what my wishes are, as I have already said ; and I have not found it possible to resist the desire I felt to write to you. For it appears to me that if this be not done, it will be committing a great sin against God, against the King, our lord and father, and against your Highness, whose life and royal estate may our Lord guard and increase.

"Richmond, 25th October."

But in the beginning of 1508 the painful truth appeared in the letters of King Ferdinand. The Archduchess Margaret had merely refused to marry, but the Queen Juana had still a husband. The body of Philip had been embalmed and went about with his wife. Ferdinand wrote that he would do all in his power to promote the marriage, but he must tell the King of England that the Queen of Castile carried the corpse of her late husband about with her. No one was able to prevent it or to contradict her. On New Year's Day she had insisted that the same honours should be paid to the dead Philip as would have been paid to him alive. Ferdinand had to put off initiating any discussion of a new marriage till the ceremonies were over; even then she had begged that nothing should be done till her late husband was buried. But she refused to bury him. Ferdinand wrote to the Pope asking him to intervene by letters: he himself looked forward to exercising slow persuasions. Meanwhile all was useless. Six months later there had been no change, and the hopes and intentions of the Tudor in Spain were defeated by that embalmed body of the unburied dead. He had sent enough to the grave; he had been in that very June planning to send others "without warning." The grave left its inhabitants on earth to reject him.

Thereafter the two old and intimate friends and adversaries, Henry and Ferdinand, returned to the one unfailing subject of dispute. On 15th July 1488 the amount and payment of the marriage portion of the Princess Katherine had been first discussed. On 7th August 1508 Ferdinand was still sending directions about it. "In all these matters," he said, "Henry has shown extreme covetousness and but little love" (love!). He was inclined to break entirely with the Tudor. "All this I say, because, in treating with people of no honour, and indifferent character, it is necessary to take care that we receive no injury and that we are not cheated." Nor did his imagination stop there. The King of England had been suggesting that Katherine's marriage portion should be settled on himself. Ferdinand thought it politic to agree, but the twenty years' old distrust broke out. After so many years, after so many letters, the King of Spain felt himself defeated financially—for both him and Henry almost the worst defeat of all. He was pricked by the poison of defeat; if the money were settled so, he wrote, "they would perhaps poison her to get possession of it." Three and a half centuries afterwards, it is not possible to feel quite certain such a thing would have been beyond the ageing malevolence of the King's accumulative mind. It would have been a great treasure to add to his already great treasure. Ferdinand thought him capable of it, and Ferdinand was no fool. Between Henry and Ferdinand the suspicion lay, and there is little evidence to suggest which of them was the most capable. The King of Spain wrote on: "It must be seen to that the term of years fixed upon be the longest possible, in order that there may be time for the bearing of children, and for giving the King leisure to get rid of his fancies and ill-will, and to be freed from the temptation of killing the Princess of Wales."

Letters from Membrilla bitterly complaining of the Princess of Wales and of her confessor, letters from the Princess of Wales bitterly complaining of the ambassador, came hurrying across to the old man, but he had no care to attend to them. His thoughts were on the other man in England, who had beaten him on the money, and who (therefore) might murder for it the Princess of Wales. That other man himself was concerned with his own fixed illusions of policy. He was still only fifty-two; he was still thinking of marrying the Archduchess. He had lost ground a little in diplomacy; he needed to regain it. In August and again in October he dispatched new embassies into the Netherlands. He sent one of his younger men, the latest of those political ecclesiastics he had used so often, a full-blooded ambitious active creature of thirty-three, his chaplain, Thomas Wolsey. Wolsey had been a Fellow of Magdalen, and rector of Limington; afterwards he had been made chaplain to Archbishop Deane, and from there had come into the King's household. He had done one job in Scotland satisfactorily; now he was hurried off on the new errand. He was sent to the Low Countries, to talk with the Bishop of Gurk. If the Bishop would support Henry and help gain him the hand of the Archduchess, Henry in turn promised that he would make the Bishop a chief man in the Netherlands. The Archduchess was not to be moved, but none of them believed it. On 5th November 1508 the King of England wrote " to our trusty and well-loved clerc and chapelain Maister Thomas Wolsey," of things that might be done, " the said marriage once concluded betwixt us and the said duchesse of Savoye, and the rule and governaunce being committed unto us and the said duchesse."

The corpse of King Philip had defrauded Henry Tudor of one alternative; the Archduchess remained firm long enough to deprive him of the other. She had no need to do it long; soon he was deprived of all. In the early part of 1509 he fell ill again. Food became repulsive to him. Before Lent opened he made promises of political reform, to examine into the deeds of "all them that were officers and ministers of his laws." He promised to issue a general pardon, to cease from persecuting the rich. The consumption gained on him. In March he was worse, at the beginning of April he was in serious danger. He was then at Richmond, in his new palace. He became so feeble that they dared not give him the Sacrament. He had it brought in the monstrance into his chamber, and prayed and wept. He received extreme unction. But apart from these rites, his death keeps itself as hidden as his life. By the 20th of April he was almost dead; he lay in a state of extreme weakness and pain, for more than a day and a night, crying on God, possessed (but more than any?) by deep fears. On the 21st of April they said before him a Mass of Our Lady, "to whom he had always a singular devotion," and later in the same day he died.

John Fisher, preaching over the dead body of the King, said : " And or we proceed any further . . . let us here devoutly and effectually say for his soul and all Christian souls, one paternoster." And paused till it was done.

CHAPTER X

The Conclusion

THEY brought him first from Richmond to St. Paul's; afterwards from St. Paul's to Westminster. He was solemnly interred in the state of the Kings of England; he had desired and determined that life and death, and that was given him. The procession through the City was very magnificent. The Swordbearer of the City headed it, with representatives of the Crafts; then came the royal pageant. The King's messengers, his trumpeters, his minstrels; the foreigners—presumably the ambassadors; chaplains and squires of the Body; aldermen and sheriffs; heralds and the King's Steward, with knights following; chaplains of dignity (such as Deans); the King's Council, Knights of the Garter, the Judges. After the lay the spiritual procession. " Then came the Crutched Friars on foot, and all the four Orders of Friars followed, singing. Then the Canons of all the places in London, singing. Then the King's Chapel, in their surplices and grey amices, singing." Then on horseback, the lords temporal on the left, spiritual on the right. Three knights followed, bearing the helmet, the axe, and the armour. The Lord Mayor. The Hearse : drawn by seven horses in black trappings, each with a knight on either side; covered by a cloth of gold on four staves, and a lord bearing a banner at each corner. The car itself contained the coffin, with upon it a picture of the dead King in his state, a gentleman usher at its head and another at its feet.

Nine lords followed, and nine "henchmen," three of whom bore the three Caps of Maintenance sent by three Popes. The King's Horse. The Guard and many gentlemen. The worshipful men of the Crafts of London. The Lords' servants, "being a great number."

"Thus and in this manner was the said corpse of King Henry VII brought through the City of London, with torches innumerable, unto the West Door of St. Paul's, where the Bishop of London, revested and mitred, received the said corpse." On the next morning they sang three masses, and the Bishop of Rochester preached, "which done every man departed unto their dinner." Afterwards the processions reformed and went down out of the City, along Fleet Street, to Charing Cross, and so to Westminster, where four abbots, all the convent of Westminster in albs and copes, and presently the two Archbishops, received the body.

On the third day three more masses were sung

and in the third offerings were made, first by all those who carried any armour or properties of the dead King ; then by the lords and gentlemen on their own behalf. The mass was ended and a sermon preached by the Bishop of London.

They drew to the end. The King's Chapel broke into the anthem *Circum dederunt me gemitus mortis*. The Archbishops, Bishops, and Abbots came down to the hearse. " And then the said corpse was incensed, and all the royal ornaments taken from the said corpse, so that every man might see the said corpse coffered in a coffin of boards, which was covered over with black velvet, having a cross of white satin from the one end of the said coffin unto the other ; within the which coffin the very corpse of the King lay enclosed in lead. Upon the which lead was written, in great letters chased, *Hic jacet Rex Henricus Septimus.* And so the said corpse was laid into the vault with great reverence by the noble Queen Elizabeth his wife ; whom incontinent all the Archbishops, Bishops, and Abbots setting their crosses upon the said corpse assoiled, in most solemn manner saying this collect : *Absolvimus.* Which done the said Archbishops did cast earth upon the said corpse. And then my Lord Treasurer and my Lord Steward did break their staves, and did cast them into the vault ; and the other head officers did cast their staves in, all whole. Which done the vault was closed, and a goodly rich pall of cloth of gold laid upon the said hearse. And incontinent all the Heralds did off their coat-armour, and did hang them upon the rails of the hearse; crying lamentably in French, *The noble King Henry the Seventh is dead.* And as soon as they had so done, every Herald put on his coat-armour again, and cried with a loud voice, *Vive le noble Roy Henry le VIIIth;* which is to say in English tongue, God send the noble King Henry the Eighth long life. *Amen.*"

He had established power and again organized kingship. In order to do this he had to be there; it was his first achievement—he was. Secondly he had, with whatsoever motive, to act at once dangerously and discreetly; he did. He made England quiet, and he made it quietly. The later Tudors—even Elizabeth—were louder and less composed. True, Elizabeth had a more difficult time; she had to deal with religion where her grandfather had only had to deal with property. He did; he managed it so well that by the end of his reign it was indeed his property. He left it to his son, and his son lost it. He might well have turned in the tomb of his spoiled chapel at Westminster, could he have seen the cause of that loss: the throb of a spiritual fear, the itch of a fleshly nerve. He himself was not so fretted by texts or tantalized by faces. In so far as he lost control, it was within himself, and (as it were) causelessly ; at least, he only lost it to his old self.

He had always defended and encouraged the trade of England ; he had loosed the white sails on the sea, and built other ships to protect them. But these, as the new century proceeded, were rather the sails of the merchants than of the King. The trade he had encouraged betrayed him, and those other white things, the sheep in the fields. An Italian traveller wrote of the English : " They have an extraordinary number of sheep," long before Thomas More's macabre comment : " Sheep are eating men." In 1490 there had been an attempt to defeat the sheep in the Isle of Wight and to maintain the smallholder. There the destruction of farms and the growth of large estates had already been observed. Men were disappearing from the island, and it was given up to cattle and the rich. But it failed. Of the mainland itself it was soon to be said that where there had been churches and religious houses " you shall find nothing but sheepcotes and stables to the ruin of men." The nibbling four-footed innocents advanced over the country like the locusts over Egypt. They nibbled, and the smaller farms and houses disappeared. The larger farms, the greater houses, took in the lesser lands ; it was the process of nature and of economics. The wool trade and the cloth trade—quarrelling sometimes between themselves—became prosperous; manufacturers and merchants throve; it was the process of nature and of economics. Even King Henry could not stop the sheep, but his multiplied eyes had watched and his multiplied hands had wrecked the huge houses that were already beginning to rise on those moving backs. It did not last; English wool stifled the English Throne. But at first there was nothing but pleasure. The miserly, ageing, unjust King was dead, and there was to be a new King and a new day. There was a great treasure to be spent. There was to be spectacle and culture and learning and a great glory. There were to be masques and triumphs—perhaps the finest masque and loudest triumph was to be a grand war, after so many years' peace. Dudley and Empson were put to death; the persecution of the rich was stopped. Suffolk, for safety's sake, was still kept in the Tower. Erasmus was to be recalled to England. More and Wolsey and the new Henry Tudor were equally free and prepared to be equally glad. At the opening of all the gorgeousness—on 11th June 1509—King Henry the Eighth permitted himself to forget his protestation, and (under advice of the clergy) to marry the Princess of Spain. On 31st January 1510 her first child was born—dead.

BIBLIOGRAPHICAL NOTE

THE chief modern studies are *Henry VII*, by James Gairdner (1902) ; *England under the Tudors : Henry VII*, by W. Busch (1895) ; *Henry VII*, by Gladys Temperley (1914) ; the essay by Dr. C. H. Williams in *The Great Tudors* (1936), and another by Professor Conyers Read in *The Tudors* (1936).

Among the sources used are the State Papers of the period ; the histories by Polydore Virgil, Hall, and Holinshed ; the volumes of Campbell's *Material for the History of Henry VII* ; and of Gairdner's *Memorials* and *Letters and Papers* (both for this and the next reign) ; Oppenhein's *Naval Accounts* ; the *Italian Relation* ; Leland's *Collectanea* ; Bentley's *Excerpta Historica* ; the Paxton, Plumptre, etc., *Correspondence* ; Kingsford's *Chronicles of London* ; Tawney's *Tudor Economic Documents* ; *Transactions of the R. H. S.* (N.S. xvi–xviii) ; Stubbs's *Medieval and Modern History ;* and, of course, Francis Bacon.

INDEX

A

Alexander VI, 87, 120, 126, 130, 141, 142, 223, 230.
Andreas, Bernard, 168.
Angus, Earl of, 161.
Anne of Beaujeu, 73, 88.
Anne of Brittany, 17, 76; duchess, 78, 85; marriage, 86.
Arthur, King, 54, 57.
Arthur, Prince, 53, 54, 78, 175; marriage, 79, 83, 141-2, 156-8; letter to Katherine, 155; death, 158, 210, 214.
Ayala, Pedro de, 144, 162, 163; on Henry, 147, 163.

B

Bacon, Francis, quoted, 19, 33, 59, 61, 98, 167, 174, 205, 208, 211, 214, 219-21.
Beaufort, Margaret, 8, 53, 65; marriages, 1-3, 14; and Buckingham, 15-16, 19.
Boleyn, Anne, 68, 234.
Bolton, William, 176.
Bosworth, battle of, 29-30, 33, 36, 59, 61.
Bothwell, Patrick, Earl of, 161, 164.
Bray, Sir Richard, 213.

Brittany, Duke of, 10, 73; and Henry, 10-14, 17, 21-2, 23.
Buckingham, Edward, Duke of, 32, 38, 68, 161, 195.
Buckingham, Henry, Duke of, 14, 18-19.

C

Cabot, John, 167, 183.
Capell, Sir William, 216-17.
Cassel, Provost of, 207, 248.
Chambers, R. W., 179, 217.
Charles V., 75, 246, 247.
Charles VIII, 73, 86, 88; and Warbeck, 107; in Italy, 120.
Claymound, 153.
Clifford, Sir Robert, 112.
Colet, John, 129, 179.
Columbus, Bartholomew, 183.
Cornish rebellion, 133, 139, 141, 211.
Crusades, 190, 248.
Curzon, Sir Robert, 190, 197.

D

Desmond, Earl of, 106, 107, 136.
Dorset, Marquis of, 19, 23, 65.
Dudley, Edmund, 96, 214, 215, 218-21, 264.
Dunbar, William, 164, 168.

E

Edward IV, 4, 5, 7, 10, 13, 90.
Elizabeth, Queen, 7, 70, 114, 134, 147, 168, 174, 236, 262.
Elizabeth, wife of Edward IV, 16-17, 21, 23, 64.
Elizabeth, wife of Henry VII, 11, 16, 32; and Richard III, 21, 24-5; prisoner of Henry, 33; marriage, 48, 52; coronation, 53; children, 53-4; and De Puebla, 101; at the entry of Katherine, 157; and the death of Arthur, 158-9; More's poem on her death, 169; tomb, 177; death, 227.
Empson, Sir Richard, 96, 214, 215, 218, 219-21, 264.
Erasmus, 179, 180, 181-2, 250, 264.
Estrada, Duke de, 223, 224, 226, 228, 235.

F

Ferdinand, King of Aragon, 9; and the marriage of Katherine and Arthur, 79-83, 141, 156; war with France, 82, 83, 84, 162, 225; and De Puebla, 100, 102, 143; and Warbeck, 109, 110, 122, 123, 124; letters and pensions to non-nationals, 161; and Scotland, 162; marriage of Katherine and Prince Henry, 193, 224, 229-31; and Suffolk, 194, 223; as Regent of Castile, 243, 246-7; and Henry's own marriage, 247, 251, 253-4; last quarrel with Henry, 254-5.
Fisher, St. John, 1, 175, 258, 260.
Fox, Richard, Bishop of Exeter and Durham, 40, 43, 82, 96, 134, 163, 180, 213.
Frampton, Sir Edward, 105.

G

Gordon, Katherine, 127, 128-9, 137.
Guelders, Duke of, 197.
Guildford, Sir Richard, 188-9.
Gurk, Bishop of, 256.

H

Hampton of Worcester, 168.
Hanse, the, 111, 196.
Henry V, 2, 24, 30.
Henry VI, 2, 3, 4, 7, 10, 93, 166; and Henry VII, 6; translation, 177, 178.
Henry VII, parentage and birth, 1-3; attainder, 4, 6, 41; and Henry VI, 6; escape, 8, 88; proposed surrender, 11; offer of the Crown to, 17; marriage to Elizabeth of York, 17, 18, 20, 21, 48, 52; first attempt at invasion, 18; head of the Revolt, 20-1; flight to France, 22-3; lands in England, 27; Bosworth,

INDEX 269

29–31; in London, 35; his royalty, 37, 41, 49, 90, 166; piety, 39, 69, 152, 166, 175, 190, 248–50; coronation, 40; restoration of royal power, 44–7; and money, 59–60, 140, 214, 225, 254–5; Northern progress, 61–3; Simnel, 63–71; marriage of Arthur, 72, 78, 79, 141–2, 156–7; and Maximilian, 74, 83, 123, 125–6, 194–5, 245, 246, 247; and commerce, 75–6, 111, 196–7, 263; Brittany, 76; and war with France, 76, 77, 82, 84–7, 126, 142, 146; and the people, 90, 174, 219; spies, 97, 112; and de Puebla, 98–102, 143–4, 225, 226; and Warbeck, 103–4, 110–14, 134, 136–7, 149–54; and Scotland, 123, 137–8, 161–5; accedes to the League, 126, 130; persecution of the rich, 131, 215–7, 218–21; Cornish rebellion, 132–4; accounts of, 139, 147, 152; exchanges with Spanish sovereigns, 142–3, 145, 224; court and behaviour, 166–84, 209; and learning, 168, 180; architecture, 175–9; will, 175; as a father, 180, 235; the the pursuit of Suffolk, 186–90, 192–7, 205–6; and a Crusade, 190, 248–50; and King Philip, 204–6; his enemies, 207; and Prince Henry's marriage, 224–7, 229–31, 234; proposals for his own second marriage, 227–9, 235–42, 245–8; and Katherine, 243–5, 247, 251; final diplomacies, 256; death 257; funeral, 259; supersession, 264.

Henry VIII, 52–3, 92, 151, 166, 206; birth, 54; superstition, 69; Duke of York, 112, 187; devotion, 178; and Erasmus, 181; marriage 193–4, 224–7, 229, 232–4, 245, 264; Prince of Wales, 227; and his father, 235; accession, 262–4.

I

Innocent VIII, 51, 68–9, 92.
Isabella, Queen, of Castile, 9, 79, 109, 124, 231; exchanges with Henry, 142, 143, 225–6; death, 202, 243; and King Henry's marriages, 228. See Ferdinand, King of Aragon.

J

Jacob, Henry, 172.
James I of England, 183.
James I of Scotland, 72–3.
James IV of Scotland, 55, 72; and Warbeck, 107, 123, 127, 135; invades England, 129–30, 135; peace, 137; marriage, 163–4; and Suffolk, 197.
Juana of Castile, 202, 243, 246–7, 250–1, 253–4.
Julius II, 231, 249.

K

Katherine of Aragon, 55, 56, 69, 192–3; marriage with Arthur, 79–83, 141–2, 146, 155–8; and De Puebla, 100, 102, 244; with Henry VIII, 224–7, 229, 230–4, 255, 264. her distresses, 243–5; complaints of the ambassadors, 244, 255; letter to Juana, 252.
Kildare, Earl of, 106, 136.
Knights of Rhodes, 249.

L

League against France, 123, 124, 126, 130, 141, 142, 162.
Londoño, 143, 144, 146.
Louis XI, 11, 88.
Louis XII, 245, 248.
Louise of Savoy, 246.
Lovell, Lord, 61, 62, 65, 70.

M

Margaret of Angoulême, 245.
Margaret, Archduchess, 207, 245, 246, 256, 257.
Margaret Beaufort, see Beaufort.
Margaret, Dowager-Duchess of Burgundy, 33, 34, 62, 65, 104; and Warbeck, 108, 110, 119.
Margaret, Princess, 54, 123, 163–4, 218.
Mary, Princess, 54, 247.
Maximilian, Emperor-elect, 73–4; and Henry, 83, 110, 141, 194–5, 248; and Warbeck, 108–9, 110, 119, 121, 122; disowns him, 125–6; and Suffolk, 191, 194–5; and Henry's marriage, 246, 247.
Medina del Campo, treaty of, 84, 87, 96.
Membrilla, Knight-Commander, 244, 255.
More, John, 217–18.
More, Sir Thomas, 15, 156, 217, 263; poem on the Queen's death, 169; and Henry VIII 181, 264; on Morton, 211.
Morton, John, Chancellor and Archbishop, 15, 19, 41, 43, 50, 96, 130, 144; and Richard III, 22; return, 40; and Reform, 131, 180; character, 180, 208, 210–12; Morton's Fork, 212.

N

Naples, Queen of, 235–42.

O

Oxford, John de Vere, Earl of, 23, 221.

P

Paulet, Quintyn, 172.
Pepys, Samuel, 179.
Peter the poet, 168.
Philip, Archduke of Austria, 76, 108, 161; King of Castile, 198, 202, 243; in England, 202–6, 246; death, 246, 253.

INDEX

Pius III, 230.
Pole, Edmund de la, Earl of Suffolk, 186; trial, 187; first flight, 188; second flight, 191; with Maximilian, 194; James of Scotland on, 197-8; proposes terms, 200; surrendered, 206, 264.
Pole, John de la, Earl of Lincoln, 19, 32, 65, 70, 186.
Pole, John de la, Duke of Suffolk, 40, 185-6.
Pole, Richard de la, 198-200, 208.
Pope, *see* Alexander VI, Innocent VIII, Julius II.
Puebla, Rodrigo Gonsalvi de, 82, 98-102, 124, 141-6, 224; quarrels, 143; on Warbeck, 149-50, 154-5; and Scotland, 162; and Prince Henry's marriage, 226; and the King's marriage, 228, 235, 251.
Pynson, Richard, 172.

R

Richard III, 13, 15, 18, 20, 45-6, 49, 79, 90; proposed marriage with his niece, 21, 24-5; and Henry's invasion, 27-9; at Bosworth, 29-30.
Richard, Duke of York, 106.

S

Sanctuary, 62, 91.
Simnel, Lambert, 64, 70, 81.
Skelton, John, 168.

Stafford, Sir Humphrey, 61, 62.
Stafford, Thomas, 61, 62.
Stanley, Thomas, Lord, 14, 19, 25, 28-9, 59; at Bosworth, 29-30; Earl of Derby, 38, 40, 115.
Stanley, Sir William, 25, 26, 28; at Bosworth, 28-30; and Warbeck, 113; executed, 114.
Star Chamber, 91-6.
Steelyard riots, 111.
Stoke, battle of, 67.
Surrey, Earl of, 67, 85.
Symons, Richard, 64, 70.

T

Temperley, Gladys, 91, 196, 218.
Tudor, Edmund, 1, 2.
Tudor, Jasper, 3, 4, 5, 7; in Brittany, 8, 23; Duke of Bedford, 38, 40.
Tudor, Owen, 2, 4, 178.
Tyrrel, Sir James, 188, 193.
Tyrrel, Sir Thomas, 119.

U

Urswick, Christopher, 22, 76, 77, 79, 126.

V

Vertue, Robert, 176.
Vignolles, Bernard de, 115-9.

W

Warbeck, Perkin, origin, 104-5; in Ireland, 106, 122, 136;

in France, 108; with Margaret of Burgundy, 108; in Austria, 110, 119; and Clifford, 112; off Deal, 121; in Scotland, 123, 127; his marriage, 127–9; invades England, 129, 130; leaves Scotland, 135; lands in England, 136; taken, 137; comment on, 140, 151; a prisoner, 149; flight, 150; arraignment, 152–3; execution, 154.

Warham, William, Bishop of London, 260, 261.
Warwick, Richard, Earl of, 21; prisoner of Henry, 33, 64, 81, 149, 151; **arraignment**, 152–3; execution, 154, 180.
Westminster, Lady Chapel at, 175–9.
Wolsey, Thomas, 181, 213, 256, 264.
Woodville, Edward, Lord, 77, 78.

www.ingramcontent.com/pod-product-compliance
Lightning Source LLC
Chambersburg PA
CBHW030136170426
43199CB00008B/88